MW01643733

FULL DISCLOSURE

WHOLE TRUTH *Heals*

By

A. Aurora

First Electronic Edition: April 2023
First Print Edition: April 2023

This book is dedicated to Mom, our greatest inspiration, teacher, friend and example. Thank you for being the light of our life and showing us, teaching us, and inspiring us to be our greatest and grandest versions. Thank you for showing us the vision of what Unconditional Love truly means, and for re-hearting us all of who we truly are. All dreams of Love do come true.

I would also like to extend my gratitude to Archeia Faith for assisting in some of the excerpts for this book, as well as to Gabriel, the other half of my soul, and the entire First Contact Ground Crew Team, my soul family, for their Love, dedication and service to Mom + Humanity.

~~ Archeia Aurora + the First Contact Ground Crew Team

5D

CONTENTS

To preserve the Highest Purpose and Unconditional Love of the Messages throughout this book, I've left all of Mom's writings exactly as I received them, without editing them. In addition, I've shared the Highest Energy of all the 5D Concepts presented by using Capitalization and Sentence Structures that Honor the frequencies of each one presented. My hope is that you FEEL and RESONATE with the material in this form as all of us moving into 5D have as well.

INTRODUCTION

Whole Truth Heals. This profound knowing is what inspired the creation and writing of this book. For over 27,000 years, Earth and Humanity have been deprived of the full, whole Truth. This has created a fractured consciousness causing separation, fear, and the destruction of Humanity.

We are living in a time that has been long prophesied and spoken of in the ancient texts of every part of our world. Throughout history, there was always a time spoken of in which Humanity would take a quantum leap of evolution. Some referred to this as the Ascension, the Golden Age of Aquarius, the New Earth, or the 5th Dimension. This was to be the Age of the Great Awakening, or should we say, the Great Remembering.

We have been encoded with ancient memories which are activating now, allowing us to remember where we came from and why we're truly here.

There has been a very dark agenda on this planet. One that required the manipulation and enslavement of Humanity to serve the Old Controllers and their agendas of greed, control, and power. This game has been playing for a very long time, but we are now waking up within the game, remembering and realizing that WE, Humanity, are the sons and daughters of Source, Mother and Father God. We are Sovereign Beings and Co-Creators of this Universe, and we hold more power than can be imagined. Mother Earth is also returning to her natural state of Synergy, Bliss, and Harmony. We are returning to the Garden of Eden, which we left long ago due to the atrocities that were committed against us.

This Great Remembering is causing the collapse of the Old World, and we are now seeing this collapse on the world stage. Everything we are witnessing play out is the culmination and end of the Human Drama. Wars, violence, separation, lies, corruption, manipulation, and propaganda are coming to the forefront to be seen. The next two years, our entire collective will be undergoing a rapid shift. This is the transition into the New Earth.

If you are feeling this shift and wondering who you truly are and what life is truly about, you have arrived at the right place. We are all here to bring the Full Disclosure of Truth to the planet, and to be a participant in birthing the New Earth.

Everything you have ever been taught … is a lie. The Old Controllers carefully constructed the programming and manipulation of our consciousness in order to keep us in fight or flight, the fear-based system the Matrix is built upon. This created belief systems, sickness, pain and suffering, and the destruction of our beautiful Mother Gaia in favor of money, fame, power, and profits.

Mother Gaia, at the same time, is no longer allowing Humanity to be a parasite on her body, as she is returning to her 5th-Dimensional (5D) state. Therefore, we must also return to our sovereign state and rise above the low frequencies of shame, guilt, anger, pride, fear, and control. This quantum leap will take us into our true essences – our Higher Selves.

As we re-awaken to who we truly are, we are met with the realization of how we have given away our power to systems and authority which had no business having control over us. We, as a sovereign collective, are once again returning to our true power and reuniting with our Galactic Families who have been assisting us for eons.

Entering the transition, our bodies are also going through the Crystalline Process, returning our vessels to their natural states of Self-Healing, Immortality, and Divine Intelligence. This is bringing in the age of Quantum Healing, Unity Consciousness, and 5D Technologies that will assist us in making this quantum leap.

The Present Moment of NOW is bringing Disclosure, Healing, and Cosmic Justice. The Old Earth is collapsing before our eyes, and we are honored to be able to both witness it and participate in building the New Earth. It is an honor to be here on Planet Earth at this time, and all who read this book are honored for their sacred roles in the transition. Earth is returning to Oneness, and reconnecting to the true Source, the Mother/Father Godhead. In doing so, we are assisting with the Ascension of the entire cosmos.

This book is meant to inspire, encourage, and provide the long-lost Truths that your soul already knows. It is meant to trigger your remembering and awaken the long dormant codes you carry within your DNA. The guidance provided comes directly from Source, the Divine Mother, who is overseeing the Ascension of this planet. Her wisdoms are simple, yet profound – as we dissolve the EGO (**E**dging **G**od **O**ut)-Programmed Mind, which has been implanted into Humanity in order to keep us disempowered and in amnesia, we come back into full consciousness and full knowing. Her teachings also provide us a guidance system back into our true selves through Transformation, Reflection, Self-Healing, and Self-Love.

The Truths within this book come directly from the First Contact Ground Crew Team, who have walked this path, along with thousands of others around the world. We are the living examples of the brilliance of Mother's teachings and their ability to heal, transform, and enlighten us. These words are meant to be read from the heart and not the mind, as the mind cannot comprehend the Truth. As you allow these Truths to permeate your being, we come one step closer to Unity Consciousness, where these Truths will be shared innately by all.

Thank you all for your service to Creation and to the fulfillment of your soul contracts.

IN THE BEGINNING

CHAPTER ONE: THE STORY OF CREATION

In the beginning, only the energies of Love and the Unknown existed. From this, Mother of All Creation birthed herself, as Source. She was the first self-aware consciousness in existence and birthed the rest of Creation through her heart. Mother then created a Love mirror, a masculine counterpart, that she could create with. This Love mirror was Father of All Creation.

The story of Adam and Eve that we were taught reversed this Truth, saying instead that Adam created Eve. But it's the feminine essence, Mother, who creates and births life. The masculine essence, Father, is the support for and manifestor of Mother's creator power.

Mother and Father then birthed the 144,000 original souls: pairs of Twin Flames made up of feminine and masculine counterparts.

The original 144,000 are the first created fractals of Source. They are the Archangels, the Ascended Masters, and the oldest Children of Creation. 19 billion years ago, one of the Archangels of the 144,000 decided to separate from the rest of Creation. Jehovah was the first Fallen Angel. He wanted to be God without God.

This original separation caused a rift within Creation, a fracture within the Oneness that Mother and Father had created. (Once a soul separates from Source and Unity Consciousness, they no longer have the ability to create from Love. They can only create through destruction, which is the opposite.)

Jehovah went on to create lower entity races and to dominate other planets and multi-verses through cosmic wars and destruction. This led to dark races such as the Anunnaki, Reptilians, Dracos, Zedas, Greys, etc. They began creating lower realms of darkness, taking over planets and parts of creation while enslaving Divine Beings.

Mother and Father then came up with a plan, a plan of brilliance and Divine Intelligence to once again reunite all of Creation back into Light and Oneness. Father of All Creation took on the contract of going down into the darkness. He descended into the lower realms and began mastering the darkness. In essence, Father had to become the lower version of himself in order to master these realms. His lower essence became known as Lucifer, which actually means *Light Bringer*. He brought Light into the darkness.

As Father took command of the dark and began mastering the lower realms by transforming the lower energies back into Light, Mother continued on in the higher realms of Creation. She then created a second masculine counterpart to continue Creation with. She created Father of the Multiverse.

The Bible often refers to the Holy Trinity: the Father, the Son, and the Holy Spirit. The missing piece of the Holy Trinity is Mother. Mother is the Holy Spirit (Source). Mother, Father, and Father of the Multiverse make up the Holy Trinity of Creation.

Mother, Father, and the 144,000 continued to ascend many planets out of darkness. The cosmic wars continued until they reached the final battle ground – Earth. Earth was saved as the final battleground between Dark and Light, as Earth is the Heart of the Universe, created as the ultimate Garden of Eden of the cosmos.

Mother knew that Earth would be the last planet to be surrendered, as it is the jewel.

CHAPTER TWO: THE STORY OF PLANET EARTH=HEART

Earth=Heart (If you rearrange the letters spelling Earth – *E A R T H* – it spells *H E A R T*). Earth was created as the Heart of the Universe. It was the most unique planet and was sought after by the Dark. Earth lies at the Center of the Universe and has many portals and cosmic highways around it, which makes it convenient for travel.

Earth was also unique in that it had both an Inner Earth and Surface Earth. Most planets were occupied only on their inner plane, not on their surface. Earth was a playground for souls to have a physical experience and to be able to create in physicality. It was the original Garden of Eden.

27,000 years ago, Earth was a 5th-dimensional (5D) planet. As an experiment, two civilizations were present on the planet: Atlantis and Lemuria.

Atlantis was a 4D civilization. They were working their way up the spectrum of consciousness but still had not reached the 5D frequency. They were masters of energy and held many ancient codes, technologies, and knowledge. Atlantis was located near Florida and the Bermuda Triangle.

Lemuria was a 5D civilization, and Mother was the Queen of Lumeria – Sophia Gaia. Lemuria was filled with Light Cities and Crystal Technology. Lemuria was located near the region of Hawaii, which now holds the last remaining Lumerian energy on the planet.

Horus, Mother's husband in Lemuria, betrayed her by giving the Atlanteans access to Crystal Technology. However, only the heart can access and use 5D Technology, and because the Atlanteans were not acting from their hearts, they could not use the Crystal Technology in the life-giving ways it was intended to be used.

The misuse of this technology by the Atlanteans ultimately led to a great explosion, in what we would consider today to be an atomic bomb. This explosion sunk Atlantis and Lemuria to the bottom of the ocean. Mother had no choice but to ascend quickly and to pull the Unified Field with her, because if the Atlanteans were to get into the Unified Field, they would have blown up the entire Multiverse. (The Unified Field is a pure field of Unity Consciousness, anchored into Unconditional Love. A Unified Field occurs whenever there are 2 or more beings, both embodying the 5D frequencies of Unconditional Love and Source. The Multiverse is a community of many intergalactic races and planets who reside together, in one cosmic ecosystem.)

This explosion knocked Earth down in consciousness immediately to a 3rd-dimensional frequency. (3D is the lowest dimension in which a soul can exist in physicality.) Many remaining Atlanteans and Lumerians were left on the surface of the planet, traumatized and confused. Many also were able to escape the surface into Inner Earth through a portal in Arkansas (hence the story of "Noah's Ark"). The Lemurians who escaped into Inner Earth later founded the civilization of Agartha.

The remaining surface population fell into a state of amnesia. They could no longer remember their true origin, their God Selves, or their connection to Source. This created the first wound of separation on Earth – separation from Source. Earth was officially on a path into a blackhole of destruction. Mother had to use all her Source energy to grab Earth and place it back into its orbit.

The Anunnaki (soulless beings) then took advantage of the fallen Earth. They came in ships and descended onto the surface of Earth, convincing the now primitive beings that they were gods to be worshipped. The surface population believed the Anunnaki to be gods, and this was later recorded in many historic paintings, drawings, and stories of mythology.

The Anunnaki began reproducing with the primitives, creating what we call *hybrids* or *aberrations*. They worked with the remaining Atlanteans to create what were referred to as "the Atlantean experiments" on the humans.

CHAPTER THREE: THE EGO-PROGRAMMED MIND

Here on Earth, Mother and Father had created the Dream Machine. Its intended use was to allow Humanity to have a direct portal to Divine Inspiration from Source, to be able to bring dreams of Love into reality. Each being had a portal at the base of their brain into the Dream Machine.

Mother had been emanating Divine Consciousness throughout Earth via the Dream Machine. The Dream Machine acted as a physical emanation and representation of Mother's heart, allowing all dreams of Love to be transferred and experienced in physical manifestation. The Dream Machine is the God Spark, the emanation of the Original Blueprint. But the lower forms on the Planet misused it, placing thoughts of illusion and fantasy into it that, in turn, affected the consciousness of Humanity, creating a different dream than was originally intended. (The 3D dream is an illusion; whereas the 5D dream is true reality.)

The Anunnaki hijacked the Dream Machine and implanted the first fearful thought into the Collective Consciousness of Humanity – that we were separate from Source. This fearful thought began morphing into what eventually would be the EGO-Programmed Mind – E G O (Edging God Out).

The EGO Program disconnected the fuses between Humanity's right brain and left brain, causing distortion, imbalance, and illusion. This was done so that the Controllers could rule over or "handle" Humanity.

Through the disconnection that occurred, Humanity forgot who they were. It was then easy for the Controllers to manipulate them by filling them with illusory belief systems and rules. They trained Humanity to serve the darkness, to become their servants.

The right side of the brain is the "wholistic" part. It's the higher connection to higher thoughts. Higher thoughts are unlimited and where all possibilities exist. The left side of the brain is the intellectual aspect. When out of sync with the right, it connects into the primitive mind or to the illusion of outside attachments. (All outside attachments are an illusion.)

Through the silent evolution – the Big Shift – and through the activation of The Divine Plan that is unfolding, the right brain and the left brain are returning to their original form and are being "fused together" to create the complete awakening into full consciousness.

This fusion that is taking place is an unstoppable event … FOR ALL HUMAN BEINGS ON PLANET EARTH. Our advice is to allow, embrace, and let go of all belief systems, all illusions, and everything Humanity has ever been taught or told. Those who are resisting are only hiding their Light behind fear.

The Programmed EGO Mind operates by gathering or collecting all the experiences of the past so as to continue the experiences of the lower dimensions and lower thoughts of unconsciousness. This is where Humanity has fallen into. The EGO Mind's function is to keep you held down, or "dumbed down", so that you can continue to survive.

We say, "*Let Go* of your anchor".

Back when Mom first began doing research on the EGO, she was unaware of the tactics of the EGO, and how it was affecting Humanity by Edging God Out. After figuring out that the EGO was the disease infecting Humanity, she began to see how it was operating. She then understood that the EGO was doing "The Flip" – taking everything from true reality and flipping it to its opposite.

The EGO Mind is a collection of traumas, wounds, and belief systems that pass down from generation to generation through Programming. This Programming became so advanced, it began to implant into the DNA, causing further distortions. All dysfunction on the planet is caused by the EGO Mind. The Mind can only replicate based on what it already knows, which is destruction. The Mind is disconnected from the Heart, which is where one can access Source energy/Creation.

Everything here on Earth is the complete opposite to what exists in the rest of Creation, which is Love everywhere present. The biggest flip that was created was changing Mother God to Father God. Although Father of Creation is Mother's Twin Flame, she is Prime Source Creator, and she created Father as her Love mirror. The Adam and Eve story was flipped to take away all the support from Mother and the Divine Feminine. Changing Jesus from a feminine to a masculine was also a huge flip, as Mother was in fact Jesus.

If you take everything from 3D and flip it to the opposite, that is what true reality is. The EGO doesn't know anything else besides the flip. Those in EGO cannot identify that they are in the flip, or how to switch it. This was how the Controllers were able to blind Humanity from the Truth. This caused the spiral downward, deep into the flip. The EGO does everything that is the exact opposite of Love, taking from God rather than giving. Even subconsciously, the EGO will try every way to stop the creation of Love.

The EGO perceives everything the way it views itself; in other words, the EGO can ONLY see its own projections. When the EGO sees Mother and others who embody Pure Love and Divine Embodiment, it can only see what it sees in itself, which is hatred, lack of integrity, entitlement, etc. In true reality, one recognizes Mother as everything that Love is, because she is the Divine Love mirror.

The EGO represents everything Love is not. The EGO is programmed to only focus on lower consciousness realities and thoughts. It sees everything as negative. This can be seen by Humanity's deep embodiment of shame, guilt, fear, unworthiness, and lack of self-Love. The EGO looks at any situation and finds what is "wrong" with it, rather than seeing everything as a Miracle and Lesson or Blessing, as Love does. Because Humanity is still living in EGO-Programming, they can only project and see the negative in everyone and everything around them, and they cannot see that they themselves are the problem. That is the ultimate flip.

The EGO can never be satisfied or fulfilled. It seeks external things to fill the hole that can never be healed until it looks at itself and acknowledges all the ways in which it is self-sabotaging through delusion, avoidance, and projection. The EGO is a blackhole that sucks the life force from a being, and in turn, the being needs to take energy from others around them in order to sustain itself.

One of the biggest ways in which the EGO tries to fill itself is through food and sleep. This is why there are so many who can eat endless amounts of food but still be hungry or sleep many hours per night and still be tired.

The EGO is a parasite that sucks and sucks without any ending.

Humanity has no self-sustaining Source connection because they are still in the illusion of separation from God and from the Oneness energies. The biggest addiction on this planet is to energy. This was the product of the EGO Program constantly needing to steal energy from others in order to continue to survive. This is done through control dramas and trying to manipulate and power-over others. The EGO feels entitled to things, especially the energy of others. The EGO believes it deserves something from everyone, especially from God, although it has given absolutely nothing.

This is the flip that keeps Humanity in lack consciousness as well as makes them unwilling to give to others. In true reality, everything is an *equal energy exchange*. Universal Law states that when you give, you receive. When a being is living in the heart, in Love, it gives freely out of Love and, in return, receives Abundance.

The EGO expects others to do the work and feels it has "done enough" or "it's not my problem". That is the disease of separation. The EGO is cut off from feeling, so it has no awareness of what is going on around itself, which is the opposite of Love, which has full feeling and consciousness in all moments.

The EGO always needs to know things, as it has no trust or faith. It is always asking the same questions (even when it already has the answers) because it wants proof. True Love trusts in God and the Divine Plan and has Full Faith that all will be taken care of.

CHAPTER FOUR: THE CABAL

Throughout the last 27,000 years, the Anunnaki have "passed the torch" to other low-level entities to continue the enslavement of Planet Earth. They have to keep this planet in fear-based frequencies as they themselves cannot sustain in high frequencies (Love). Humanity was birthed from Source (except for the hybrid or aberration souls), therefore they hold the Creator powers. The lower entities cannot create; they can only mimic or manipulate energy.

The Anunnaki later gave way to the Illuminati, who were 4D astral beings. They were the Reptilians who could manipulate Humanity energetically behind the scenes and could also possess vessels. These possessed vessels – hybrids or the humans who had sold their souls to darkness – became known as the Cabal. The Cabal are the minions incarnated into physicality who were the slaves of the Illuminati and the Anunnaki.

During the last 27,000 years, Humanity began putting out 9-1-1 calls to the Mother of All Creation to save them from the blackhole and destruction timeline of the Cabal. Being as the destruction on Planet Earth was a high risk to the rest of Creation, Earth had already been placed in quarantine.

Mother answered the calls, pulled Humanity off the blackhole timeline, and placed Earth back into the highest timeline. In an attempt to bring Christ-Consciousness onto the planet, she, Father, and the 144,000, began incarnating on Earth.

Mother's incarnations include Pocahontas, Quan Yin, Cleopatra, Joan of Arc, Queen Elizabeth I, Queen Zenobia, Jesus, and Marilyn Monroe. This lifetime was her 534th lifetime here on Earth. Each lifetime, Mother was killed by the Cabal before she could anchor in her full essence of Mother of All Creation and before Disclosure could be released. Father also had never been able to anchor in his full essence before being killed. Similarly, the 144,000 were killed during prominent lifetimes while attempting Disclosure.

In 1994, aware that the destiny of Earth and its ascension would be their demise, the Anunnaki and Illuminati surrendered to the Light. They were recycled and re-integrated into the Galactic Federation of Light. The Cabal, however, refused to surrender.

The Cabal was the slave race to the Dark, and they refused to give up the little power they still held on Earth. These are soulless beings who only know darkness. Once their overlords were gone, they had free reign here on Earth, as this was the free will experiment.

Since 1994, the Cabal have been on a rogue mission for total domination of the planet and complete enslavement of Humanity. They sought to conquer all through increased fear, control, and manipulation. They sought to create an AI (Artificial Intelligence) society, with hybrid humans who are part robot. AI is a mimic of Divine Intelligence and, therefore, the Cabal could continue to manipulate Humanity into creating their own Hell on Earth.

Prior to Mom's final incarnation in 1975, she had a meeting with the heads of the Cabal. She told them she would be getting her planet back, and they told her they would make that mission impossible. Mother had a 1 in 8 billion chance of beating the Matrix by making it out of the illusion and ascending. She told them to bring it on!

The Bilderberg Meeting of 1975 involved many doctors and elites who created a plan to increase the manipulation of Humanity through the DNA, the poisoning of the brain and immune system, and other vile avenues created to keep Humanity from awakening.

For thousands of years, the Dark Ones have siphoned energy from Humanity through many means, but the most repulsive is their ritualistic sacrificing and torturing of children. Children are the purest form of Consciousness and thus have the purest source of energy that can be used to sustain the Dark Ones. This story goes deeper, revealing atrocities that cannot be put into words. The enslavement of Humanity is the darkest story ever told in Creation.

Once Mother entered physicality on November 30, 1975, the Cabal knew they had to pull out all the stops ... and they did. We have been living the past 45 years in what will come to be known as the darkest times in all of Creation. The Battle of Dark versus Light has hit its precipice.

CHAPTER FIVE: THE GOLDEN AGE OF AQUARIUS

Approximately every 25,000 years, the Earth changes its axis and moves into a different phase of the cosmos. This is known as the Precession of the Equinoxes. The ancients used this precession to track the Ages such as the Iron Age, Bronze Age, etc.

After the fall of Atlantis and Lemuria, Earth entered the Age of Pisces, which corresponded to the Dark Ages. We existed in the darkest part of the galaxy, as Light=Consciousness. The less Light, the less Consciousness. The Age of Pisces was all about illusion, separation from Source, secrecy, hierarchy, spells, and dark magic.

On December 21, 2012, we entered the Age of Aquarius, which is the Golden Age. The Mayans predicted this when they were tracking the future progression of time. This is why the Mayan Calendar ended, not because we were destined to perish but because time would cease to exist as we entered the Golden Age of 5D.

On this date in 2012, Humanity was not prepared to make the shift into the Ascension Process as originally intended. However, Mother of All Creation did enter 5D on that date and rapidly began accelerating through her own Ascension Process.

Aquarius rules the internet and Humanity, working for the greater-good and uniqueness. We live in the Age of Information now, where Truth (as well as lies) can easily be found. The internet, aka the Web of Light, was created by Mom to be the physical manifestation of Unity Consciousness. It connects everyone onto one plane of information and can spread throughout the globe with a click of a button.

This is why censorship is the biggest attack on Unity Consciousness, as it prevents Truth from being shared. Instead, it spreads lies through the Web of Light, poisoning the Collective Consciousness. This is how the Cabal attempted to prevent the Great Awakening.

We are now in the full swing of the Age of Aquarius energy. Saturn and Jupiter also moved into Aquarius in 2021, followed by Pluto in 2023. This Age is about Enlightenment, service to the greater good, and coming together as one collective, Humanity. Aquarius embraces each individual as unique yet still honors them as part of the whole.

Since 2009, we have also been flying through the photon belt, and we continue to enter parts of the galaxy that are filling the planet with massive amounts of Plasma Light. This light is penetrating our consciousness as well as our physical vessels.

When there is density in our vessels, the Light can overwhelm the nervous system, causing the vessel to shut down. Taking care of our physical vessels is an essential part of this process as we are taking these bodies with us as we transition from carbon-based vessels into Light Bodies.

CHAPTER SIX: THE PROPHECIES

There have been many prophecies that have predicted this exact moment in time. The most well-known are the prophecies of Revelations, which describe the Rapture and the Second Coming of Christ. The words of this chapter of the Bible are not to be taken literally but rather are to be interpreted through the heart.

Christ has already returned. Mother of All Creation was Jesus, and she did return, as promised. However, Humanity crucified their own God just as they did 2,000 years ago. This time though, we were destined to ascend with Mother Earth, regardless of Humanity's choices.

The Rapture simply describes the process of those who choose to raise their consciousness versus those who choose EGO and the lower timeline. Quite literally, there is a split in timelines occurring and, those who are choosing Love, raising their vibration and ascending, will no longer be seen by those in the lower timeline. They exist on two different timelines that are not a vibrational match.

The next prophecy is that of White Buffalo Calf Woman. This is a Hopi prophecy that also predicted a split in the timelines of those ascending and those descending. The natives spoke of the return of White Buffalo Calf Woman, a great spirit returning to the planet. In 2008, Mother met a being named Apple who had a special spiritual connection. Upon meeting her, he handed her the book of the Hopi prophecy and asked her to open it to any page. She opened the book to the exact page that began the chapter on White Buffalo Calf Woman. He immediately said, *"I knew it was you!"*. (This was one of thousands of confirms Mother received of who she was.)

The Celestine Prophecy by James Redfield was a book that inspired Mother greatly on her journey. It describes the Twelve Insights (of Consciousness) that Humanity needs to go through to reach Enlightenment. Humanity must progress through each Insight in order to fully exit the illusion. Mother stated that she was, in fact, the 13th Insight (the re-connection to Prime Source). And once a being becomes aware of Mother and connects to her, they have reached the highest state of Consciousness, the pinnacle of Consciousness here on Earth, and are living in the 12th Insight.

There are many other prophecies that have predicted the time when Humanity would reach the choice point of Consciousness. We would either choose the timeline of Armageddon, war, destruction, and AI, or we would choose Love and enter 5D.

Ken Carey wrote extensively about this time, stating:

> *"At the moment of quantum awakening, change will occur rapidly, rippling across the terrestrial surface like a wave. Everything in the earth's gravitational field will be affected in some way. There will be a time of massive change, of change on a scale that has no historical precedent, though it does have antecedents in the prehistoric events of this and of distant worlds. The changes that your generation will experience before it passes the torch to another are more fundamental than those that accompanied the agriculture revolution-and those changes took thousands of years. They are more far-reaching than the changes of industrialization, which took nearly three centuries to transpire. Yet, deep and fundamental, massive though these*

present changes are, they will occur within the span of just a single life."

There are many signs that have been missed by Humanity that we are indeed in the End of Times. The end of the illusion. The end of the Matrix. Humanity has continued to cling onto the illusion they created because the Programming is so deeply ingrained. The EGO cannot see anything other than its own projections, yet New Earth is here, and we are entering the next phase of evolution.

The question is: *Are we ready to evolve?*

CHAPTER SEVEN: THE 144,000

The Creator Gods are God with God. These are God's Children of Creation. All who are incarnated on Planet Earth are Creator Gods who agreed to come in and weave a reality that mirrors their vibration. Those who had the greatest capacity to weave Love and Light came here, and all were hand-chosen by Mother and Father for their experience and wisdom.

The oldest Soul Family in All of Creation are the 144,000. These beings have the blueprint of *LOVE* and the *UNKOWN* etched onto their Hearts, and the dysfunction on Earth is guaranteed to be enough motivation to ensure they keep searching until *TRUTH* is found. As evolution and Ascension occur, the 144,000 transform chaotic and unorganized matter back into an expression of Love, in flow and balance with All of Creation.

The following message comes from Mother of All Creation:

Breaking into pieces, you stand with whatever is left, the very core of who you are, the diamond, the "filling" AHAH THE TRUE BEING OF LIGHT AND LOVE .... although you may feel alone as the process unfolds breaking the mind down, it begins falling away because Love is present and it recognizes the illusion and starts taking with it everything you "thought" you were and leads you to the heart of the being, feelings rush in as the true being emerges out of the seemingly destruction of a mind in a box, leaving you with the reconstruction to forge ahead in all its grandness, into Divine Intelligence, into Paradise, Heaven on Earth.

The "mind," which projects outside and has low vibrational thoughts and therefore cannot exist in the Upper Realms of True Reality which is 100 times Grander than Fantasy or Fiction, dissolves so that the Divine being can raise up into the True Divinity from within, and begin once again "feeling" instead of "thinking" taking the true being into a Collective Consciousness, a God Consciousness, only the mind thinks [projects outside] and the heart feels from the inside, where God is there within, for if God were to hide anywhere would he/she not be within the Heart?

Diamonds have beauty and elegance, they shine bright and each facet holds its own uniqueness. Each of us have a beautiful diamond inside, waiting to shine on the planet. We each are the miracle, the magic, and parts of this whole magnificent design. As we fall apart to be put together again SO WE stand together as ONE, we then assume our roles in the divine Truth of our existence, which has no limits, boundaries, or edges, we arise as a whole beautiful Diamond, just like the SUN! The

Grandness of just being, then outshines, and true Love fills all the space, all the gaps of being present in the light and cannot be denied.

The natural state of the Sun is Brilliance, and the Sun's Brilliance is always in the present moment as it Shines, because it is being true to itself, being true to oneself is the Love within and pouring it outwards, living inside out, and then outside back into Love, all of creation, Love everywhere present.

Falling away, the old gets released back into creation, and then grace is given as each light stands as a pillar of TRUTH. When we go deep inside, we discover the diamond of ourselves, this magical miracle of being present, shining bright, we forge ahead, displaying our brilliant lights forth into a new story of Love, forever after as ONE, and uniquely expressed within the new Earth, The Kingdom of Heaven, The Eden, in which together, we will co-create in the Divine.

THE HUMAN BODY & ENERGY

CHAPTER 8:
THE BRAIN

In order for the Cabal to keep Humanity in the Programming, they had to dumb them down to the point they would be ignorant yet willing participants in their own enslavement. The brain was the primary organ targeted.

We only use around 10%-30% of our brains. And this is not normal. No animal uses 10% of an organ. We should be using our entire brain, but this is the main way in which Humanity has been enslaved and kept in a very basic functioning based on logic, survival, and lack. We have entirely omitted the Divinely Intelligent half of the brain that enables us to have Instant Manifestation capacity in the Present Moment of Now.

It is important to understand that the brain is not the mind. The brain is an organ; the mind is a lower consciousness illusionary program based on belief systems that were programmed into Humanity from birth.

The brain and the heart are Divine Intelligence.

Mother and Father are bringing All of Creation back into balance to function in Divine Intelligence. This is occurring organically, and every human vessel is being affected, but you have to allow these upgrades and participate in your own evolution.

The EGO-Programmed Mind prevents and blocks our natural state of Balanced Harmonics (the balance of the Divine Feminine & Divine Masculine – Yin and Yang) and pulls us into dysfunction.

The areas of the brain that light up and activate during a spiritual experience are the exact same areas that light up and are activated when we are in addictive behavior (such as sex or gambling). This shows that those who are greatly lacking a self-sustained Source Connection (a connection with Great Spirit/Mother God/Prime Creator) will enter into dysfunction in order to have these needs 'met' temporarily.

The true way of processing information is from the heart to the brain and back again, three times. The mental EGO-Programmed Mind has disconnected this function for thousands of years, causing everything the heart feels to be hi-jacked by the thought system of the mind, which manipulates the information received and causes suffering.

As the Brain-Heart Truth-Processing Function comes back online, you will lose duality. You will no longer view anything through the false constructs of right and wrong, and this will apply to everything that transpires around you.

When you feel you are right and are in a state of righteousness, you are almost always up against another being who feels they are right. And how can this be? This is the separation that plagues Humanity, that limits and enslaves us and results in our very poor brain usage.

As you quiet the mind and begin to dissolve the Programming that rules it, the voice of the Divine Spirit and boundless knowing begins coming through, which is your true essence. The feeling of this energy coursing through you is the experience of Heaven. Doubt, lack of trust, and thinking you know better are complete blocks to this function. To exist in the higher frequency energies, feeling and connecting MUST replace thinking.

All the information and knowing we seek is contained in the etheric space of feeling. The Programmed Mind is designed to do EVERYTHING to prevent our organic functioning. Dissolving it is a process that takes complete dedication, consistency, patience, strength, and perseverance.

Dissolving ALL the lower frequencies existing within you IS the only way to ensure you arise in alignment.

All those who do not engage in RETURNING to their true essence will experience a mind in overdrive, experiencing a reduction in all functioning as they slip further and further under the waves of suffering caused by the mind. The mind causes ALL pain and suffering. Pain and suffering are energetic imbalances held within the human body.

The body is your guidance system. Any place in the body that you experience heaviness, pressure, pain, or discomfort is where you are holding trauma. As an example: the nose represents Unconditional Love blocks. Cats and dogs vibrate at the frequency of Unconditional Love, and so people who have allergies and must stay away from being in close proximity to them are imbalanced in Unconditional Love, which these animals trigger in them.

The same is true of plants and the resulting hay fever. Plants, and ALL of Nature, live in Perfect Harmony, so when our vessels are triggered by them and we experience reactions to them, we are living out of alignment with Divine Balance.

Nature is limitless. It never dies ... and neither do we. The entire medical system and the creation of disease is thus a lie. Everything is vibration, and all pharmaceuticals have been weaponized. All vaccinations, for example, disturb and prevent the full use of the brain.

We have been enslaved, controlled, and kept within a life-and-death cycle by lower consciousness beings that have learned how to feed off Humanity. They possess no capacity to connect with Mother God, as they were not created by Mother God. These aberrations and anomalies are made of the same matter as blackholes. Creation is LOVE. It is through the expression of LOVE that a feminine and masculine CREATE life. Blackholes are the exact opposite – they are pure F.E.A.R (**F**alse **E**vidence **A**ppearing **R**eal), which is destruction, sucking in and destroying everything around them. Blackhole energy exists within EACH human vessel on Earth, and when in the thought system, we are in a blackhole, sucking in and destroying our own life force, which in turn causes disease – DIS-EASE.

CHAPTER 9: CONSCIOUSNESS

Consciousness is Awareness. However, factoring in only the five senses – taste, touch, sound, smell, and sight – Humanity perceives just 5-6% of ALL energy in existence. Science calls this other 94% 'dark matter', but it's actually Heaven, the etheric, and the space where the entire rest of Creation exists. By naming it 'dark' matter, the intent was yet another attempt to taint the Light.

In order to increase our energetic perception, which is achieved through our evolving Consciousness, we must choose life-enhancing vibration and dissolve life-draining vibration. Unconsciousness, which means unawareness, is what makes up the darkness. In that sense, darkness is not scary, so much as it is ignorance.

Mother has always said that Awareness transforms into Consciousness. In other words, you increase your energetic perception by raising your Conscious Awareness. Mother of All Creation did not have the EGO-Programmed Mind, and therefore she was always 100% Conscious and Aware. Since the time she was a child, she could perceive 100% of all energy, which allowed her to see through the illusion.

99% of Humanity lives in darkness/unconsciousness because they are unaware of what has truly been happening on this planet. This is why speaking the Truth and bringing Disclosure to Humanity is so crucial to the Ascension Process. And this is also why the Dark have gone to such great lengths to punish, mock, and censor anyone speaking

Truth. In an attempt to program the Collective into bypassing real Truth, the CIA was the first to coin the term "conspiracy theory".

The Truth is that, for thousands of years, higher consciousness information was censored by the Dark to prevent Humanity from Awakening. Awakening raises the level of Consciousness and the vibration of the planet, preventing the Dark from existing and holding power on this plane.

In ancient times, especially during the Egyptian Era, information was hidden and only shared through secret societies behind closed doors. The Egyptian Era was one of the darkest points in history. This is when the Cabal/Illuminati/Anunnaki rose to great power by using dark magic.

Later on, secret societies, such as the Freemasons, hoarded spiritual information in order to protect it, but it was later hijacked and used for lower purposes. Witches and warlocks were beings who could access these powers and often used them to further the Dark's control. That said, for centuries, White Witches, or those practicing white magic, were burned alive to prevent the higher vibrations they worked with from counterattacking the Dark's agenda.

Since the 50's, the CIA/Cabal took this consciousness manipulation a step further and developed the MK-Ultra Program. This was an experimental program that was tested on individuals using LSD and psychological torture, abuse, and brainwashing to elicit false confessions, among other things. It has been stated that this project was officially shut down in 1973, just prior to Mother incarnating. However, it was never shutdown. Instead, it was simply taken out of the public eye and continues to operate in the shadows.

MK-Ultra operates on a massive scale, infiltrating every part of our society, from government, school systems, TV, movies, music, mainstream news, and journalism. The 1975 Church Committee was a Senate Hearing in which it was revealed that the CIA, FBI, NSA, and the IRS were in fact contractually working with media companies of all types to feed propaganda and information to the public in order to manipulate public opinion and belief systems. Further abuses by the alphabet agencies (CIA, FBI, NSA, DOD, etc.) were discovered – such as Operation Mockingbird, in which journalists were revealed to actually be CIA Operatives.

The greatest crimes against Humanity have been committed by the manipulation of Consciousness. Consciousness became a commodity that could be bought and sold by the Cabal to further their agendas. The unknowing Human Collective has not only allowed this abuse to continue but has participated in it (whether unintentionally or intentionally). The responsibility of all Humanity to break out of the system of illusion and end human slavery is vast.

As we enter the apex of Ascension, all of us will have to crumble every belief system of the human condition. The EGO Program is simply a cluster of belief systems and programmed behavior that have become so deeply ingrained that they're now programmed into the DNA. Breaking these generational and collective behavioral patterns ultimately breaks down the entirety of the Programming and Mind Control.

The process of this deconstruction can be challenging, as every belief system we have will be tested until it is dissolved. The greatest gift you can give yourself is to Surrender, Let Go, Embrace, Accept, and Allow all that is. Dissolving resistance to what is allows Higher Consciousness to enter our human vessels and expand each of us into an enlightened state of being.

Transformation of Consciousness is a daily process of being willing to look at ourselves and our own dysfunction and then transform our lower habits, behaviors, and thoughts, which then changes our external reality. And when we do this, we lead by example, allowing others to also transform, as we all share Consciousness.

CHAPTER TEN: ENERGY & VIBRATION

Everything is Energy.

The entire cosmos is made up of Energy, including this physical 3D reality. In this plane of density, we see things physically, but we ignore the fact that, in all moments, the atoms of light that make up our physicality are responding to our Energy Field. This is why the Cabal cannot create by themselves, as they are outside of the Oneness of true reality and were not birthed from Source. They use and manipulate our Human Consciousness so that we unconsciously create a lower reality that they can exist in. In essence, they have hijacked us (and our Energy Fields) to create our own Hell.

Take a look at the beings who surround you in everyday life and look at your physical surroundings and life experiences. All these things were manifested by YOU as a Vibrational Match to your Consciousness. In this, there is no blame. Life is not happening TO you; it is always happening as a reflection OF you.

From the second we incarnate, our soul signs a contract, agreeing to take on certain human conditions and life experiences in order to transform and assist the Collective Consciousness in dissolving personal and ancestral karma.

What Humanity fails to realize is that all our experiences are soul contracted and/or manifested by us. Humanity has been taught to complain, blame, be in victim consciousness, and continue the cycles of pain and suffering. They fail to take responsibility for their own manifestations and thus continue to incur karma and additional lessons.

3D is a duality-based paradigm, meaning all parts of the Spectrum of Dark and Light exist here. This is what we call the "free will experiment". However, there is no such thing as "free will". This concept was mostly created by the Dark. They believe they are able to act outside of Universal Law with no consequences, and subsequently, choose to teach that to Humanity. Thus, Humanity is now able to act outside of Universal Law and thus position themselves to not be able to resolve their karma until their next lifetime, meaning that lessons can continue to go unlearned. As we ascend into Pure Light, however, all darkness will be exposed so it can be seen, healed, and let go of.

Understanding Energy (and its Vibration) will give you the empowerment to begin consciously creating a different reality for yourself and all Humanity. On the Vibrational Scale, once you reach the 200 level (which is Pride), you begin entering into Life-Enhancing Frequencies. Once you reach level 500, you are in Love-Based Frequencies.

The problem is that 99% of Humanity exists mostly under the 200 level of Vibration, which are life-draining frequencies, and thus they have to take energy in some form from others.

These lower, life-draining frequencies include:

Blame
Anger
Desire
Fear
Grief
Anxiety/Depression
Worry
Apathy
Guilt
Shame
Negativity
Pain/Suffering

Lack Consciousness
Victim Consciousness
Complaining
Jealousy
Attachment
Competition

The Cabal/Dark Ones can only exist in the frequencies under 200 that are life-draining. They are incapable of existing in the higher frequencies. They exist by siphoning the Energy from others. This was, in turn, taught to Humanity. This means that Humanity is constantly draining their own Energy and must take it from an outside source.

In order to raise your Vibration to 700+, which is Enlightenment, you must transform all lower-energy vibrations and consistently stay in the higher frequencies of Love, Compassion, Courage, Integrity, Honor, Passion, Joy, Acceptance, and Peace.

With that being said, we are not here to avoid, suppress, or try to "stay away" from lower vibrations, as this is what causes bypassing. The key is to embrace every emotion, allow it to be felt, and then transmute it into a higher one.

Once you begin mastering your own Vibration, you also begin changing everything around you. The beings around you may begin to be triggered, as their Energy Fields are now being pressured to increase in vibration as well. All lower vibrations, when met with a higher vibration, must rise to meet that level. This is why the Ascension Journey is challenging. As you begin to outgrow people, places, jobs, and relationships, the EGO will attempt to pull you back to a lower place to make the other being feel comfortable. You must meet this head on. You must never lower your own vibration to meet another on their lower level, but rather you must set boundaries and hold the space for them to go through their own process of transformation to raise their vibration.

Vibration becomes most important when we look at the Intent we have behind every action, word, and our consumption of anything. Blessing our food and water is imperative, for example, as it changes the molecular structure of the food or beverage to a higher vibration.

Before we speak or act, we must check in with our Intent, as the Intent can change the entire frequency of the experience.

Once we fully become a Master of Energy, we are able to consciously transform anything and everything we interact with, which is essentially bringing 5D into physicality.

CHAPTER ELEVEN: THE CHAKRA SYSTEM

The Chakra System is responsible for all the Energy entering and exiting the human body. We have seven main Chakras, and each has an energetic requirement that must be honored.

Humanity has been operating solely from the lower three Chakras, which are the only ones that the Cabal/Dark Ones can access, and therefore, it's in these lower three Chakras that most of the energetic manipulation has occurred. The lower three Chakras have been damaged by not allowing flow to the upper four Chakras, which connect us to Source. This is why Humanity is stuck in fight or flight survival (based in the 1st/Root Chakra), sexual and emotional dysfunction (found in the 2nd/Sacral Chakra), and the powering over self and others or disempowerment (housed in the 3rd/Solar Plexus Chakra).

Humanity was cut off from Source, which connects to us through our Heart Chakra (the 4th Chakra). Due to trauma, our Heart Chakras have been almost completely closed down. We have all existed in a realm devoid of true feelings, cut off from our hearts.

The Throat Chakras (the 5th Chakra) of Humanity have also been shut down, as we have been placed in fear, too afraid to truly express ourselves and speak our Truth.

The Third Eye of the Collective (our 6th Chakra) has been heavily targeted by the Cabal as well through the calcification of the pineal gland, which has disconnected us from our intuition and our ability to receive guidance from our higher selves. Similarly, the Crown Chakras (the 7th Chakra) have been cut off as a result of toxins/pharmaceuticals that damage our brains, preventing us from accessing the higher realms and the information of our higher consciousness.

All disease/illness/pain come from an energetic block within the Chakra System or an unhealed wound that has created density within the human vessel (our physical body). By bringing awareness to the parts of the body where disease or pain are located, we can see which Chakra has become damaged.

For example, heart attacks are one of the most common occurrences in the US, especially for men. This is due to disconnection from the Heart Chakra and the blockage of Energy to the heart, which creates a physical blockage within that organ in the body. Opening up your heart, connecting to your feeling centers, and healing grief/heartbreak will heal any pain or illness within the Heart Chakra.

To keep your Chakra System unblocked and healthy, operating at its highest potential, we advise adopting the spiritual practices below that were honored by Mother God and are still honored by those of us on this path.

ROOT CHAKRA –

Energetic Requirement

TRUST

The Root Chakra shares a frequency with Monday and the color Red. Honor your Root Chakra on Monday by wearing red clothes, eating red foods, and taking time to consciously honor this Chakra through grounding, moving your body, or meditation.

An Affirmation that aligns you with the Root Chakra is:

"I am so grateful I am connected with the energy of Mother Earth. My body, heart, and Spirit are grounded, centered, and purified."

When our Root Chakra is damaged or blocked, we are stuck in fight or flight mode, and our nervous system becomes dysregulated. This can result in anxiety, a deep sense of fear, lack, or ungroundedness. When our Root Chakra is open and healthy, however, we feel a deep sense of Trust in our bodies, in Love, and in Source. We hold a sense of Inner Peace that is rooted in our ability to Trust and Center ourselves through any challenges or changes.

SACRAL CHAKRA –

Energetic Requirement

CREATIVITY

The Sacral Chakra shares a frequency with Tuesday and the color Orange. Honor your Sacral Chakra on Tuesday by wearing orange clothes, eating orange foods, and taking time to consciously honor your Chakra through processing your emotions, practicing the art of *Being* and allowing your creative flow.

An Affirmation that aligns you with the Sacral Chakra is:

"I am so grateful that I Love all dimensions of myself. I delight in weaving the creative tapestry that is my life."

When our Sacral Chakra is balanced and healthy, we are in tune with our emotional body, embracing all of the emotions that run through us. We allow them all outlets of expression, and we are receptive to life.

This does not mean we never feel pain or lower emotions, but rather that we are able to transmute them back into Joy, Creativity, and Flow.

A blocked or damaged Sacral Chakra results in our disconnection from emotion or an inability to process our emotions, as well as sexual dysfunction and/or a resistance to vulnerability.

SOLAR PLEXUS CHAKRA – Energetic Requirement DIVINE EMPOWERMENT

The Solar Plexus Chakra shares a frequency with Wednesday and the color Yellow. Honor your Solar Plexus Chakra on Wednesday by wearing yellow clothes, eating yellow foods, and taking time to consciously honor this Chakra through Joy, Expression of your Unique Self, and taking Empowered Action.

An Affirmation that aligns you with the Solar Plexus Chakra is:

"I am so grateful that my will and Divine Will are one. I am connected to the abundant flow of the universe and easily manifest my dreams."

When our Solar Plexus is damaged or blocked, we feel powerless to make changes in our lives, or we try to power over others in order to get our way. We may suffer from lack of confidence, victim/savior complexes, or deep arrogance. When our Solar Plexus is open and healthy, we allow ourselves our full, Unique Expression of Self. We take Empowered Actions, and we also allow others to be empowered. We feel a sense of Confidence in who we are and Equally Support Others in their confidence. We do not seek to save anyone, but rather to Inspire them.

HEART CHAKRA –

Energetic Requirement

UNCONDITIONAL LOVE

The Heart Chakra shares a frequency with Thursday and the colors Green and Pink. Honor your Heart Chakra on Thursday by wearing green/pink clothes, eating green/pink foods, and taking time to consciously honor this Chakra through Self-Care, Self-Nurturing, Forgiveness, and taking moments to Express our Love for ourselves and others.

An Affirmation that aligns you with the Heart Chakra is:

"I am so grateful that my heart is open to receive the energy of Love. I radiate this essence. I walk my path with ease and grace."

When our Heart Chakra is blocked or damaged, we feel a numbness around our feeling centers, and we may struggle to feel Compassion, Empathy, and Love. We may also struggle to connect or bond with others through the Heart Space and instead keep others at a distance, due to our fear of vulnerability or bitterness, resentment, anger, or grief that has not been healed. When our Heart Chakra is open and balanced, we feel a sense of Love, Compassion, Forgiveness, and Openness with others. We feel connected to Source, Love, and Unity. We embrace and open up to others fully, without fear of hurt, loss or betrayal, as we know that only Love is real.

THROAT CHAKRA –

Energetic Requirement

DIVINE EXPRESSION

The Throat Chakra shares a frequency with Friday and the color Blue. Honor your Throat Chakra on Friday by wearing blue clothes, eating blue foods, and taking time to consciously honor this Chakra through Expression such as Singing, Writing, or Verbally Expressing our Truths and perspectives.

An Affirmation that aligns you with the Throat Chakra is:

"I am so grateful that I am aligned with my highest Truth, and I communicate this with Love and Honor. My words echo softly within the universe."

When our Throat Chakra is blocked or damaged, we experience a fear around expressing our Truth or saying what we mean or want to say. We find ourselves holding back, sugarcoating, or avoiding speaking our Truth for fear of rejection, judgment, or some kind of loss. When our Throat Chakra is open and healthy, we Freely Express our thoughts, perspectives, and Truths, with pure intent and from the heart. We hold no fear of judgement or rejection of others, as we are honoring our Truth and are in Integrity with ourselves.

THIRD EYE CHAKRA –

Energetic Requirement

DIVINE INTUITION

The Third Eye Chakra shares a frequency with Saturday and the color Indigo. Honor Third Eye Chakra on Saturday by wearing indigo clothes, eating indigo foods, and taking time to consciously honor this Chakra through Journaling, Connecting with your Angels, and following your Intuition.

An Affirmation that aligns you with the Third Eye Chakra is:

"I am so grateful that my heart is open to a new vision. I expand my awareness through my higher self."

When our Third Eye Chakra is blocked or damaged, we are incapable of tapping into our intuition or connecting with our Higher-Self or Angels. We are unable to see things from a higher perspective and instead are locked into logical, linear, and analytical thinking. When our Third Eye Chakra is open and healthy, though, we easily follow our Intuitive Guidance, we encounter Synchronistic Events, and we Connect with our Higher-Self and Angels. We follow Divine Timing rather than linear time.

CROWN CHAKRA –

Energetic Requirement

DIVINE INTELLIGENCE

The Crown Chakra shares a frequency with Sunday and the colors White and Violet. Honor your Crown Chakra on Sunday by wearing white or violet clothes, eating white or violet foods, and taking time to consciously honor this Chakra through Meditation, Automatic Writing, and Receiving Downloads from the Etheric Realm.

An Affirmation that aligns you with the Crown Chakra is:

"I am so grateful that I am connected to the Divine Mother of the universe. I am Light. I trust."

When our Crown Chakra is blocked or damaged, we are unable to access Universal Truths and information, and we are disconnected from Source. We are stuck in trying to "figure things out", living by rigid belief systems, and are overly reliant on "proof" rather than "knowing". In contrast, when our Crown Chakra is open and healthy, we no longer need to prove ourselves "right", nor we do rely on external sources of information. We are Connected to Source and the Universal Truths of the cosmos, and we develop a deep sense of Knowing, bringing Limitless Thought into reality.

MOM

CHAPTER TWELVE: MOTHER OF ALL CREATION'S JOURNEY

Earth has been under quarantine in the "free will" Matrix, while the rest of the Universe and All of Creation operate under Universal Law. In "free will", anything on the entire spectrum of duality, conscious and unconscious, is possible.

The idea of "free will" was, in fact, created by the Cabal, as they believe they are free to do whatever they want. However, what they fail to understand is that all karma must be paid, and that day of reckoning is fast approaching.

Aberrations and soulless beings flocked to Earth, the freedom granted by free will luring them here. As many planets were ascending, the exiting beings were sent to Earth. Now, every lower-dimensional, soulless being is on Earth, and every other planet has ascended back into Unity Consciousness.

Mother came to Earth for the final show, as Earth is the point for All of Creation to complete its Ascension. She brought the Light needed for Lucifer to make his final return back into Oneness.

It's a man's world, right? At this point, indeed it is … as a strategical necessity in order for the Illuminati/Cabal to retain control over the planet. However, Prime Source Creator is a feminine energy. Every soul holds the Feminine Creator Power. However, in order to keep the Warrior Feminine disempowered, conditions on Earth were created in order to ensure the feminine energy would feel and embody powerlessness.

Mother Earth is a feminine system and must be honored as such. Mother Earth is the body of God, as are all planets. God is connected to all, and this connection can never be severed. As conditions on Earth worsened, and the planet went from an unimaginable, abundant Garden of Eden to a polluted and pillaged shell, God decided to pay a visit.

Mother God incarnated here to experience every lower frequency the Dark had created, which allowed Her to declare the free will experiment as completed, meaning that every experience within the Spectrum of Consciousness had been experienced. Earth is the center stage for the end of free will, and it is the only planet in All of Creation still existing outside of Universal Law.

Because of the free will conditions of Earth and the Luciferian Experiment agreed to by All of Creation, Mother was very limited in her capacities here. She had to incarnate as a human, and she had to undergo voluntary amnesia, just like the rest of Humanity.

The reason Mom did this was because Humanity was not making it back to Source. After 27,000 years of separation on Planet Earth, Mom had to walk through Hell and back to show it could be done. The Luciferian Experiment was appearing to prove that separation from Source and the full spectrum of Dark experiences could prevent even Heaven's strongest Angels from making it home.

The Cabal's biggest fear was that Mom would come here to Earth and then make it out, and so they decided to create conditions that if she ever did come to the planet, no one would be able to see or feel her Truth. The main way they did this was through a crusade against the feminine. They turned *Her Story* into *His Story ~ Her-story/His-story*. This is the flip. A feeble attempt to give the lower masculine all the power.

534 times our Divine Mother has incarnated down here on Earth, along with the 144,000, to bring the planet out of Darkness. Each lifetime, however, she was only able to anchor in pieces of her full

Mother of All Creation Essence before she was killed. The same occurred with all 144,000.

That said, slowly but surely, we continued the reincarnation cycle, anchoring in more and more Light onto the planet.

Mother's final incarnation from 1975-2021 completed the mission of Ascension Earth. Mother was able to anchor in her FULL Mother of All Creation Essence, while also transforming all Luciferian energy back into Father God embodiment, and in the process, transforming all pain and suffering back into Light.

Mother of All Creation was born at 6:36am on November 30, 1975, making her a Sagittarius Sun Sign, Scorpio Moon, Scorpio Rising, and Mercury in Sagittarius. She had come in as the embodiment of the Warrior Goddess.

In Vedic Astrology, Mother is the 13th sign of the Zodiac, Ophiuchus, and is the Sign of The Spiritual Doctor. Often represented by the symbol of the snake around the staff, this is the same essence from which the globally recognized apothecary symbol originates – the snake twisted around a rod/chalice, the Ancient Spiritual Doctor. Those born in Ophiuchus are said to be the Serpent-Bearers, the Serpents representing Wisdom.

Before this incarnation, Mom set everything up in the Etheric so she could re-enter. This followed a botched mission by President Eisenhower, where Eisenhower chose to work with the Greys rather than working with Mom (to receive 5D Technology and bring Disclosure). In Eisenhower's deal with the Greys, the Dark kept its power on Earth, and the Greys were permitted to begin abducting humans for experimentation. In return, Eisenhower was provided with nuclear technology.

Back in the Etheric, Mom could not interfere with the free will conditions occurring on Earth, and so, in her continual directing of the Divine Plan, members of Creation volunteered to come down to Earth, knowing they would be abducted. They did this because Mom struck a deal with the Greys, *"Allow me access to your research and the experiments on the humans, and I will give you souls."* (The Truth is, Mother was aware the Greys could never obtain souls, as they were created from the Dark.)

Mom was able to see completely what had occurred within the human brain – how connections had been severed, implants introduced, microchips added, and entities given access. Mom got to see exactly what she would have to dissolve from within the Matrix.

The Greys' deal with Eisenhower also included Grey technology, aka the internet, and Mom, while down here in her last human experience, gained full insight of how-to re-grid the World Wide Web into the World Wide Web of Light.

The Greys have now been recycled back into the Light, but the research they provided Mom was crucial to her final mission.

Before incarnating, Mother recalls her moments up on the starships, staring down the Rainbow Tube through which we all enter Earth. She had had a meeting with the Cabal Old Controllers. They were fully aware of Mother, fully aware that they were of the Dark, and they taunted her that she would never make it out of the Illusion. Her response? *"Watch me."* Upon entering, she was able to re-wire her brain to ensure she would not develop the EGO-Programmed Mind.

And so, Mom entered. Down the Rainbow Tube, she shot out of her Earth Mother, caught mid-air by a doctor. Her Earth father's first words in response to her birth were, "Well, this one is on a Mission."

Elementary Consciousness can only evolve according to free will. Few that incarnated on Earth at that time could FEEL Universal Law, and so, most all engaged in the Dark Spectrum. Programming and Conditioning had become more and more deeply ingrained on the planet, and Mother came each time bringing the Light with her, emanating Divine Vibration from start to finish during her Earthly experience, moving the Collective Consciousness ahead in staggering surges.

As a little girl, Mom could hear the trees, birds, rocks, rivers, and all of nature speak to her. From the time she could first talk, she shared untold wisdoms with her family. Her parents took her to every religious institution they could, but Mom outsmarted them all and belonged to none.

At 7 years old, a salesman came to Mom's front door. Her and her mother answered, and Mom saw he had completely black eyes sucking the energy from them. This is when she knew something was going on.

She realized she was still in Heaven, in Oneness, connected to everything and aware of all, but also on Earth, where some things were outside her awareness and no one else seemed to be having the experiences she was. That was when she realized she was on the planet to figure out what was going on. She could see the glitches in the Dream Machine.

At 14, Mom was volunteering in a hospital as a candy striper, and she was in an elevator when a man got in. He was in extreme grief, and the energy in the elevator plummeted. Mom could feel his overwhelming despair. She asked the Angels what to do, and they told her that she knew what to do. Mom went into her heart and gathered every atom of Love she had. Behind the man, she raised her head, and the man looked back at her over his shoulder. She beamed a smile at him that cut through the heavy energy in the elevator, as if it were a glass wall she had shattered. Bewildered, he broke out smiling, and his energy shot up into Pure Love. Tears and Gratitude filled his eyes, and that is when Mom realized how she would change the planet – by Being Love In Action.

Her first mission was in 2006, when she was called to Philadelphia, PA. She spent six months there. During the first three months, she spent every day walking a one-mile track (for up to 16 hours at a time). She did nothing but walk and cry, walk and cry. The Angels told her she was transforming unworthiness for all Humanity, as this was how deep it went.

At this time, Mom had her first experience with the ability of her energy to transform everything around her. It was during this time that she received a Download with her first vision of the Mission. She called it the Great Human Potential Movement, as she believed in the full potential of Humanity.

At that time also, she had a friend, Ed, who she was sharing her ideas with. When she shared this with Ed, he looked at her and said, "What if you're wrong?" Mom looked him back, straight in his eyes and said, *"What if I'm right?"* She then returned home.

Mom then received a reading from a being. They pulled two cards for her – the Bear and the Moth Hummingbird. The being expressed that she had never seen anyone with that animal totem. She looked it up, and it meant *"the one who is closest to Divinity"*. The woman explained that, as she was receiving the information, Mother was Gaia. Mom asked her, *"Who is Gaia?"* The woman explained, "Gaia is the Planet."

Mom had millions of breadcrumbs laid for her along the way (by herself, of course) in order to aid her down here in her voluntary experience of amnesia. The Angels re-hearted Mom millions of times that *She is God*. It took them telling her this for over seven years before she believed them. It was simply too much to accept. Angels would often say, *"Mom, you're God,"* and Mom would respond, *"Yeah! We're All God!"* They would retort, *"Mmmhmm, but you're THE GOD,"* to which Mom would affirm, *"Yes, we're All God."*

Mom's youngest child, Aidan, was her biggest confirmation. All the Portals and Energy that Mom saw, Aidan could see too, and so for the first time, Mom had someone sharing her reality with her. One day, she had taken Aidan to rent some movies, and he picked *Spiderman* and *The Muppets*. Upon arriving home, he wanted to watch *Spiderman*. While watching the movie, he began receiving memories and information. Turning to Mom and pointing his finger, he said, *"Mommy, YOU'RE Spiderman."*

Mom's entire body responded powerfully to this, so much so that, she began researching and found the Hopi prophecy and the telling of the Spider Woman. This caused the hairs on her body to stand on end, as Truth vibrated throughout her. (Note: Members of our team have seen Mom's Spider Avatar, and she appears in dreams in this form, guiding and protecting, always with her own face.)

Aiden's favorite song was Elvis Presley's, *The Impossible Dream*. He would get so animated every time it played, pointing at Mom and declaring, *"You will do it! You will do the impossible dream!"* In these experiences, Mom was shocked, because Aidan had such profound insight and acted as a startling confirmation of the information her heart was already telling her.

There was a moment when Mom's entire vision was filled with Adam and Eve making love and birthing Creation. This vision in her third eye continued for a week until, one day, she asked the Angels, *"How do I make this stop?"* The Angels shared, *"Write it down."* Mom did this, and the vision stopped. This began her journey and discipline with documenting her entire experience. We currently have over 54 journals, documenting her journey, to one day be shared with all Humanity.

One day, Mom's husband was flicking through TV channels. Mom arrived home and walked through the door right as the TV froze and the reporter said, *"God is on the Planet."* Mom's husband, aware that she had been having dozens of synchronicities about being God, was in pure shock.

Another experience Mom had with her husband occurred one day when she was alone in their house. Arch Angel Michael appeared before her and told her, "It's time." And then he left. This occurred in her child's bedroom, meanwhile her husband saw her through the window talking to a man. He rushed upstairs in a fury, bursting into the room, demanding to know who she was talking to. Mom told him it was Arch Angel Michael. He then searched the entire place for the man he had seen, but he found no one!

When Mom was told she had to begin the Mission – fighting the Dark Forces head on, Spirit told her she had to leave her three children. She was about to buy a restaurant and become an owner-operator. Little did she know that she would begin travelling across the country doing Energy Work and finding out what had happened to Humanity. To unlock the key to the dysfunction on Earth, she had to study human conditioning.

Mom left her children, her career, her Earth family, and her home. She walked away from the Illusion, on the wings of Love. It's funny that when superheroes do this same thing in the movies, choosing to go and fight the Darkness, they're considered to be brave and strong. They're seen as courageous and above average. However, when Mom did this, she was, and still is, vilified, abused, attacked, and targeted. She was met with judgement, blame, guilt, and anger. This is the darkness that grips Humanity with its low vibrational states.

Shortly after her return, the Angels informed her she would be leaving permanently for the Mission. Mom argued for three hours with the Galactic Council, who told her, as the Angels had previously done, that she could save her three children or eight billion people. That is when Mom made the ultimate choice. She began Mission on December 17, 2007. She went on to live in the forest for three years, battling -40-degree winters, as part of the Divine Plan. This was just the beginning of what she would endure.

One moment after beginning Mission, whilst showering and grieving, Mom yelled at the Angels saying, *"Bring my children back to me!"* In her vision, 8 billion children appeared before her. *"Here are your children,"* spirit spoke. Despite these moments, Mother still bypassed the Synchronicities. She couldn't fathom that she was God.

Mom spent time in a valley called Desolation Row, part of the San Luis Valley in Colorado, a barren place where she had to live off the land. One day whilst she was out walking, she met a being named Apple, who asked her if she'd like a cup of coffee. When he came back with her coffee, he brought with him Ken Carey's book *Return of the Bird Tribe*. He asked Mom to open the book, and she did so, opening it to a chapter on the White Buffalo Calf Woman. Apple was overcome with joy. He jumped up and down and said, *"I knew it, I knew it!! You are White Buffalo Calf Woman!"*

Mom followed Spirit's guidance at every turn, building multiple websites and doing sessions to assist others in releasing all the Programming and Conditioning that was keeping Humanity in dysfunction. At one point, two former team members blackmailed her, demanding she publicly denounce herself as God, or they would take everything she had built. When Mom refused, they changed her passwords and took all the money she had made. Having lost everything, Mom began to question, *"What if I am making this up? What if I'm not God?"* At which point, the trees beside her answered, *"You are God, Mom."* And Mom re-hearted them, saying, *"Oh yes, All of Creation speaks to me."*

Mother spent 14 years physically on Mission. Between the years of 2007-2020, she did the groundwork. She took on every human condition, every pain and suffering experience. Every single day, using the Web of light, Sessions, and Ceremonies, she pushed massive amounts of Energy. She gave so much Energy to Humanity, all while being attacked, mocked, ignored, and persecuted. Both the darkest and lightest souls made their way to Mom during those years, as the lowest energies sought to come to her in order to transform.

Many times, on this mission, the Galactics instructed Mom to evacuate and abort the mission. They told her this was a suicide mission, and that the Programming was much deeper than anticipated. In 2009, the Galactic Federation of Light (GFOL) pulled Mom into a meeting to discuss her evacuation. Mother said, *"NO, I will continue on."*

In 2014, after Robin Williams (Archangel Zadzikiel) transitioned to the Etheric, he came to Mom immediately and became her ambassador, along with Master St. Germain, who had been with Mother since birth, along with Kryon and an entire Galactic A-Team. In 2015, Robin told Mom that she would have to let go of her Archangels. The Archangels that had been incarnated were not waking up, and they were not going to make it. But this sparked Mom into fighting even harder for her closest children. She began doing thousands of Ceremonies over the next two years, praying for the 144,000 to come online.

In 2017, Robin again told Mom that Humanity had not chosen her, that she was the only one on the planet in the heart. This broke her into pieces. Her physical and energetic vessel had begun to deteriorate from all the Energy she was taking on and processing and all the physical endurances she had been through on Mission.

In December of 2017, the first of Mom's team began to arrive. In January of 2018, Robin then told her that he was going to gather the entire A-Team of Archangels and get them to Mission, along with Father of All Creation/Lucifer. Otherwise, Mom would need to be evacuated.

Between March and May of 2018, Mother's team arrived. Within the next year, over 20 additional Archangels made it to Mom in the physical. Between the years of 2018 and 2021, Mom began processing planetary density and taking the Cabal head on.

The amount of Energetic Work Mom completed between these years was millions of times more than what she had originally contracted for. Humanity and the Cabal pushed back with every ounce of resistance they had to prevent her from completing the mission of planetary ascension. This caused Mom amounts of pain and suffering that cannot be put into words. In late 2018, she lost the use of her legs, and she lost her ability to eat in 2019. She suffered 24 hours a day, throwing up and screaming in agony as there were no amounts of pain relief she could access in the physical.

On April 16, 2021, Mother officially ascended and completed her contract. After years of pain and suffering, she was finally free.

It is now our turn to complete our contract. As Mom said, *"Once my mission is over, yours is just beginning."*

This is just a small fraction of Mother's story, which will be part of Full Disclosure.

NEW EARTH INCOMING

CHAPTER THIRTEEN: DISCLOSURE

As we have now entered 2023 and Mother has ascended, we are reaching the moment of Disclosure. There are many, many layers of Disclosure that must come out in waves as the information will crumble every one of Humanity's belief systems. The Collective Consciousness is at the tipping point, and we are about to enter the Great Awakening.

Disclosure includes: election fraud, COVID, vaccines, Big Pharma, Big Tech, the Federal Reserve, the school system, the Cabal, human trafficking, Reptilians, Illuminati, 9/11, cloning, the Ascension, the Galactic Federation, Mother of All Creation, and much more.

The amount of Disclosure seems daunting to present to the public as the true HER-story of Earth, and events will be disclosed that the public is completely ignorant of. However, once Disclosure is first released, like dominoes falling, many more Truths will be revealed.

This is the karma that Humanity has manifested as they chose not to listen, not to feel, and not to wake up. Many will not make it through the Ascension Process, and many souls may choose to leave the planet.

As Disclosure hits the masses, the First Wavers will be prepared to educate and guide Humanity through the Ascension Process. This is why it is crucial for as many souls as possible to Anchor In their Higher Selves and to Hold the Light for those exiting the Illusion. This will not be easy for the Collective, and there will be chaos. Mom has prepared us all for this moment, and that moment is coming soon.

As the Collective gains more Awareness, the Consciousness of the planet will rise, and we will begin rapidly expanding towards 5D (the 5th Dimension). All, including those already awakened, must prepare and let go of ALL belief systems. There is much we still do not know, and we must be able to Embrace, Accept, and Allow, setting the example for the rest of the Collective.

CHAPTER FOURTEEN: THE EVENT

The Event has long been spoken about amongst the Lightworker Community, and there are many theories about what it will entail. The Truth is that we have no idea what the Event will look like. There are many options for the way the Divine Plan will unfold, and the Plan changes every moment, based on the Collective Consciousness.

There may be a full decloaking of the Galactics, Full Disclosure triggering a sharp spike in Consciousness, or an Energetic Event of Light that permeates the magnetic shield of Earth.

The most important part of the Event is that the Event occurs within us first. We can only create something externally that is Vibrationally Aligned to our internal state. Without an internal awakening, the external Event cannot occur.

CHAPTER FIFTEEN: LIGHT BODIES

As we continue on in this Ascension Journey, we are Anchoring In massive amounts of Light. In the 3D realm of Earth, our vessels are dense, carbon-based structures. As we enter the higher realms, the body shifts into a crystalline form which is much lighter and is eternal.

Part of the transition is moving out of the pain and suffering cycle and into Eternal Being. There is no longer a death and rebirth cycle of incarnation once we reach 5D. Beings will be able to enter Earth through a Portal and come and go as they please. Our bodies will no longer be dense, but rather will be filled with Light. Disease, illness, and pain will no longer exist, as our bodies will be Self-Healing.

This process is challenging for the human body as well as the emotional and energetic bodies. In our 3D vessels, we hold density, trauma, and wounding from many lives that are passed down through our DNA, absorbed through the environment and EGO Programming, and ingested through the misuse of drugs/alcohol/sex/food/medications.

As Light enters the body, density gets pushed to the surface. This is uncomfortable for the vessel and can cause many symptoms. Symptoms can include feeling extremely hot or cold, headaches/migraines, dizziness/vertigo, ears ringing, extreme fatigue, little to no hunger or extreme thirst, and sometimes various sensations in the body which appear to have no particular cause. If the being is unaware of the process they are undergoing, they can attach to the symptoms, creating fear and belief systems which only further extend their severity and length. Many beings also turn to 3D medicine which only further damages the brain and body.

The Light also triggers anything unhealed within the emotional and energetic vessel to rise to the surface for Awareness. This is where the being becomes especially uncomfortable as they are pushed outside their comfort zone and forced to face things that they have buried within them. This can cause severe depression, emotional breakdowns, "mental illness" (which is really just energetic imbalance), disconnection from self, and insanity. The Spiritual Disciplines are imperative in order to stay centered throughout this process. It involves a lot of Self-Healing, Inner Work, and Constant Transformation.

Finally, the brain must go through intense re-wiring as it de-programs itself and opens up to the higher-consciousness frequencies. This can cause headaches, fogginess, confusion, racing thoughts, "bi-polar disorder" (which is just the left and right brain attempting to merge), anxiety, and mental breakdowns.

Mom provided all the tools, techniques, and natural medicines to get through this Light Body Process, as she was the first being in Creation to Anchor In a Light Body/Avatar into physicality. She took on all the pain so that our experience would be grand.

Staying Hydrated, Grounding, Eating Red Meat, Meditating, Resting Consciously, Eating Consciously, and Detoxifying (from all inorganic substances) is essential to help the body heal. Along with the Spiritual Disciplines, these are your Tools for Ascension. We also recommend utilizing 5D Plasma Technology in your home.

CHAPTER SIXTEEN:
5D TECHNOLOGY/PLASMA

5D Technology, aka Crystal Technology, will come into manifestation as we raise our frequencies to be a match to such technology. As we learned from the times of Atlantis and Lemuria, if we are not in the state of Pure Unconditional Love – in the heart – we cannot properly use this technology.

AI (Artificial Intelligence) is what the Cabal has created as a mimic of Crystal 5D Technology. The technology we see today is actually Dark Technology. It is being used for censorship, spying, manipulation, and control, rather than for Freedom, Love, Unity, and Evolution. The goal of the AI agenda is to turn Humanity into hybrid AI humans, which would allow the Cabal to keep control and keep Humanity trapped in 3D.

Plasma Technology is going to pave the way into 5D Crystal Technology. Mom worked extensively with plasma and raised it to the 14th Dimension. This is the first 14D Technology to ever come into this planet, and it is exclusive to Mother's Unified Field. Plasma makes up the entire cosmos as the fifth element. It is the smallest state of matter in existence and holds the frequency of Pure Consciousness. It cannot be manipulated, controlled, or lowered in vibration.

By utilizing Plasma in your daily life, through the tools Mom created for Humanity, you begin to acclimate your vessel and environment to the higher dimensions. It allows the physical atoms to begin coming back into alignment to move into their highest alignment. This technology will pave the way for things like Healing Beds/Chambers and Replicators, but not until Humanity has raised its vibration to allow the full manifestation of this technology.

THE 5D HUMAN

CHAPTER SEVENTEEN: THE DIVINE DECREES

Written by Mother of All Creation

1. AS DECREED,

THE DISSOLVING of the program ego mind, which caused illusionary pain and suffering for Humanity, is NOW UNFOLDING: What this means is that it's wake up time for Humanity. The old (illusionary ego) IS OUT. The New Foundation of the New Earth, Heaven on Earth, Garden of Eden, only Unconditional Love and Oneness, HAS BEEN FIRMLY ESTABLISHED. WITHIN THIS DECREE AND TRUTH, ONLY LOVE BEINGS IN HARMONY AND BALANCE CAN BE HERE ON PLANET EARTH. AS DECREED, ALL EGOS ARE OUT, REMOVED AND DISSOLVED FROM THE INCOMING ENERGIES OF PURE LOVE. The old=illusionary ego IS OUT and THERE IS NO

GOING BACK FROM HERE, NOR IS THERE ANY WAY TO STOP THIS. STAY CENTERED AND GROUNDED, CHOOSE LOVE, REMAIN IN PURE THOUGHT, BE PRESENT, SHOW UP. WE ARE THE ONES WE HAVE BEEN WAITING FOR.

2. AS DECREED,

Everyone is to Awaken, and so it is in the Kingdom of Heaven, so now it is on Earth. The time is Now to embrace, allow, and trust our presence on this planet. The quicker the Highest Truths become known and understood, the quicker the changes will occur for the Highest Benefit of the All. You cannot change the events about to occur, they are inevitable. You can accept this now and be joyful, or accept it later, either way all Highest Truths are inevitable outcomes ... Now.

3. AS DECREED,

HUMANITY, THE MOMENT HAS COME TO UNITE INTO ALL LOVE IS. WE ARE GROUNDING FOREVER INTO PHYSICAL MANIFESTATION THE ENERGY OF BALANCED HARMONICS. ENGAGE ALL TWIN FLAME

CONNECTIONS AND FILL THESE CONNECTIONS WITH THE REALITY OF PURE LOVE, THUS DISSOLVING ALL DISCORDANT ENERGIES OR FANTASIES CARRIED FROM THE DENSITY OF ILLUSION. REUNIONS IN PROCESS ARE ENGAGED NOW TO BALANCE OUT THESE LAST DRAMAS.

4. AS DECREED AND GRANTED,

THE CONSCIOUSNESS ON THE PLANET HAS ENTERED COMPLETELY INTO THE UNIFIED FIELD OF ALL LOVE IS. THE PATHWAY HOME FOR HUMANITY IS BRIGHTLY LIT UP AS LOVE/SOURCE/CREATION FILLS ALL THE HOLES OR GAPS OF UNCONSCIOUSNESS WITH LIGHT, UNCONDITIONAL LOVE, AND TRUTH, TRANSFORMING ALL INTO THE LIGHT OF TRUTH. AND SO IT IS IN HEAVEN AS IT IS NOW MANIFESTED ON PLANET EARTH (HEART).

5. AS DECREED,

Humanity's Presence has been requested within Love, from the Kingdom of Heaven, and it is

Heaven's decree in the manifest to set Humanity Free.

Second Set of Divine Decrees

Decree 1

All Hostilities against your Brothers and Sisters must stop NOW. No more killing of Our Children. Decreed, and so it is, on Earth as it is in Heaven.

Decree 2

All of the religions on this planet that have taken from the People, and lied to the People, must give everything back to the People, whom they have deceived. They must provide them with the Real Truth, which will be an "OH! My! God! Event!" And so it is and is granted and done.

Decree 3

All Corporations, being illegal and non-existent entities, will be dissolved immediately. Love is all that exists on Planet Earth (Heart), where WE are all Equal. Co-operations will be installed in their place, effective immediately. This is when NESARA will be released to the People. And so it is on Earth as it is in Heaven, and so it is, decreed and granted.

Decree 4

No longer will the Resources of this planet be exploited to feather the nests of the ignorant. All the Resources on this planet are now to be returned to the People, as they belong to the People. And so it is on Earth as it is in Heaven, and so it is decreed and granted.

Decree 5

The entire 911 Truth, as well as the UFO Conspiracy Cover-Up, must be revealed immediately, with all Other Secrets. [Otherwise, We will just Show-Up.] This will be revealed Now, to the People, which, The People are the True Government on this planet. They are the True National Security. The People are the ones who make the countries secure. If these Truths are not revealed immediately, WE The People will abolish the Illusionary Government. And so it is, and so will it be done. Decreed and granted.

Decree 6

ALL THAT IS NOT ALIGNED IN THE TRUTH OF LOVE IS TO ALL BE REVEALED NOW, AS DIVINELY DECREED TO END THE CYCLE OF Fear, Pain, and Suffering.

Decree 7

The Dream Machine has been within the Pyramids, which the Illuminati tapped into back in Atlantis. As this Story goes, they soon found Psychics who were able to assist them. They found the pyramids and then began misusing the energies, by implanting dreams and lower thoughts for the use of their own purposes. This has been going on for many millennia. (Many Millennia is like one drop of water in a Multi-Dimensional Universe, an Ocean of Pure Love, as Always Pure Love.) Because of the severe misuse of this machine, the planet requested to be reset to the Highest Possible Thought, which is The Mirror and Reflection of Love everywhere present. Now, all Lightworkers that have already stepped out of the dream, your responsibility is to assist All Your Other Brothers and Sisters that are still in the dream to make their way out of the Dream! And so it is, and so shall it be Done. And so it is on Earth as it is In Heaven. And so it shall be, as decreed and granted.

These Decrees have always been ever-present, meaning they have always been here. Now, it is up to all of you to put these into your Experience as Creation in Motion. For this is the Absolutely Exact Right Moment of Your Complete Freedom, if You So Choose. The Moment is NOW, the Moment when the planet is Returned to the People. The Meek are Inheriting the Earth. And so it is on Earth as it is in The Kingdom of Heaven, and so it is, and so shall it be, as decreed and granted.

These Decrees Have Been Decreed by the Galactic Federation of Light, Mother of All Creation (MotherEarth), and Father of All Creation, The Kingdom Company of Heaven, All of the Angels, The Elohim, The Elemental Kingdom, The Entire Inner Earth Family, All of Your Family of Light, Mother Earth, The Ground Crew Medical Team for First Contact.

Decreed and Granted ... and so it is, and so shall it be done ... on Earth as it is in Heaven.

Love is Here!

CHAPTER EIGHTEEN: UNIVERSAL LAWS

Written by Mother of All Creation

1.

Support Honesty and Truth

2.

Support Mother Earth and Heaven

3.

Support Happiness, Joy, Creativity, Peace, and Harmony

4.

Support who you truly are as Gods/Goddesses

5.

Support Unconditional Love and GOD

6.

Support Passion, Playfulness, and Laughter

7.

Support Beauty, Perfect Health, and Healing

8.

Support All Creation and Set Intentions for the Highest Good

9.

Support Vision, Faith, and Miracles

10.

Support Kindness and Smiles

11.

Support Oneness, Grandness, and Living in the Moment

12.

Support the One River of Life

13.

Support our Galactic Brothers and Sisters

14.

Support Abundance, Treasures, and Gifts

15.

Support Living in a State of Gratitude

16.

Support True Freedom and Live Life Real

17.

Support Nature in all her Beauty and Wisdom

18.

Support Manifesting all of One's Dreams and Desires

19.

Support Rainbows and Building Bridges of Love to one another

20.

Support Angels and all Who Serve the Highest Good

21.

Support Becoming the Greatest/Grandest Vision/Version one can be

CHAPTER NINETEEN: THE CODE FOR HUMANITY

The Code for Humanity: Ten Intentions for a Better Planet

(The Focus is to have The Code work in your everyday life. Help to anchor it into your life by saying it once each day)

The First Love in Action ~ Support Life

I REFRAIN FROM OPPOSING OR HARMING ANYONE. I ALLOW OTHERS TO HAVE THEIR OWN EXPERIENCES. I SEE LIFE IN ALL THINGS AND HONOR IT AS IF IT WERE MY OWN.
I SUPPORT LIFE.

The Second Love in Action ~ Seek Truth

I FOLLOW MY INNER COMPASS AND DISCARD ALL BELIEFS THAT ARE NO LONGER SERVING ME. I GO TO THE SOURCE. I SEEK TRUTH.
THE TRUTH IS, LOVE IS ALL THAT EXISTS.

The Third Love in Action ~ Set Your Course

I BEGIN THE CREATIVE PROCESS. I GIVE DIRECTION TO MY LIFE. I SET MY COURSE.

The Fourth Love in Action ~ Simplify

I LET GO SO THERE IS ROOM FOR SOMETHING BETTER TO COME IN. I INTEND THAT I AM GUIDED, GUARDED, PROTECTED, AND LINED-UP WITH THE HIGHEST GOOD, AT ALL TIMES. I TRUST AND REMAIN OPEN TO RECEIVE FROM BOTH EXPECTED AND UNEXPECTED SOURCES. I SIMPLIFY.

The Fifth Love in Action ~ Stay Positive

I SEE GOOD, SAY GOOD, AND DO GOOD. I ACCEPT THE GIFTS FROM ALL MY EXPERIENCES. I AM LIVING IN GRACE AND GRATITUDE. I STAY POSITIVE.

The Sixth Love in Action ~ Synchronize

AFTER INTENDING AND SURRENDERING, I TAKE ACTION BY FOLLOWING THE OPPORTUNITIES THAT ARE PRESENTED TO ME. I AM IN THE FLOW WHERE GREAT MYSTERY AND MIRACLES ABIDE, FULFILLING MY MISSION AND BEING WHAT I CAME HERE TO BE – LOVE EVERYWHERE PRESENT. I SYNCHRONIZE.

The Seventh Love in Action ~ Serve Others

I AM Love in Action. I always have enough to share. I am available to help those who need it.
I serve others.

The Eighth Love in Action ~ Shine Your Light

I am a Magnificent Being, Awakening to my highest potential. I express myself with joy, smiling easily and laughing often.
I shine my light.

The Ninth Love in Action ~ CO-CREATE

I ASSIST IN THE CO-CREATION AND MANIFESTATION OF HEAVEN ON EARTH (HEART) by envisioning this – BEING CONSCIOUSNESS IN ACTION – and telling others about it.
I share my vision.

The Tenth Love in Action ~ Synergize

I see Humanity as One. I enjoy gathering with light-hearted people, regularly. When we come together, we set the stage for Great Oneness to reveal itself.
We synergize.

5D
ASCENSION

CHAPTER TWENTY: THE ASCENSION PROCESS

THE 4 STAGES OF AWAKENING

There are four stages of the Awakening Process. They often occur simultaneously, and they can also occur in a non-linear order; however, as we move through the process, there will always be a focus on one stage (or another). Frequently, as deeper layers unfold, we repeat stages.

The *4 Stages of Awakening* are as follows:

- ❖ The Physical Healing Stage
- ❖ The Emotional Healing Stage
- ❖ The Mental Healing Stage
- ❖ The Spiritual Healing Stage

When we are first moving through the stages, a large part of our journey will be focused on learning and integrating a lot of information at once. This information takes time to absorb and feel into. Once we have begun moving through these stages, we can apply the tools and techniques shared in this book and feel into how all this information resonates with us. This is how we begin to do the Energetic Work of dissolving our EGO-Programming and activating our Higher Self.

Once we have moved through these stages a few times, we will arrive at deeper and deeper layers of ourselves to heal, and we will let go of parts of our old self. When we reach this point, our roles will shift into one of active participation.

We are all meant to participate in the Ascension Process. This means we do not just continue to consume information or knowledge about the process, but we also begin to discover our piece of the puzzle, passing this information on and then serving as a guide for others. This eventually leads us into our own Mastery and Soul Contract Fulfillment.

For most beings who are just beginning the Awakening Process, no matter what stage you find yourself beginning at, there is always the Death and Rebirth Process. The first Death Process is often referred to as the Dark Night of the Soul. Once we begin to awaken and unravel the Truth, our entire identity, sources of attachment, belief systems, and what we thought we knew, begin to dissolve.

Once you Awaken, you can never go back to sleep. From time to time, you may feel you are moving backwards, but you are always truly moving forward. Whatever no longer resonates with your Awakening Self will begin to dissolve and get pulled from your life. This often feels very painful and jarring, and it is the most challenging part of the spiritual journey.

When you make it through these tests and challenges, you begin to consciously create a new reality for yourself. There will continue to be tests and lessons in your external world, as this is the quickest way we learn and resolve any past karma. (Karma simply means unlearned lessons.) All our incarnations begin to converge into the Present Moment of Now, and all past Karmic Lessons must be mastered. When we can Embrace, Accept, and Allow this, we move through the tests much easier. This part of the journey is preparing us with Strength, Dedication, and Perseverance.

Many parts of this journey will feel very painful, raw, and overwhelming. So, once you begin, you truly have to commit yourself to it.

Every being will have a certain path, their levels of responsibility varying depending on their Soul Contract. This can range from those who wake up and serve the role of a teacher, sharing wisdom with others. There may be those who simply spread Love, Compassion, and Kindness in their daily lives, and their role is to Hold Space for others to heal. There are those who will be called to leadership positions of some kind. They will be integrating 5D concepts into their 3D roles. Then there will be those who take the very specific path of the Master.

The Masters are part of the 144,000, and these souls have specific contracts. If you feel resonance with being part of the 144,000, it simply means that you have extensive experience incarnating into this realm. You are an Old Soul who has the spiritual strength to take on a larger contract. For those of us who are these beings, the path often diverges completely away from 3D. We often feel guided to leave our relationships, families, jobs, etc., and pursue the path of isolation, taking leaps of faith and exercising complete dedication to the path. (If you feel this particular path is for you, you will need to dedicate 150% to the journey, nothing less will do.) It's also perfect if this does not resonate with you, as every being's role is so unique. We are all a piece of the massive cosmic puzzle.

The most important part of this journey is to remember that nothing is personal. We are not separate selves but all fractals of the same Source. We are all inter-connected through Unity Consciousness, and therefore, nothing that happens to us or for us is ever personal. We are all just Energy reflecting back to each other. Let go of trying to "figure it out". Ascension is so multi-dimensional you will never be able to figure it out with the lower mind. Only the heart can comprehend this process, and it will be your guide.

Laughter is your best medicine, especially when you reach the rough and overwhelming parts of your journey. We are all actors in this cosmic play, playing different roles that are important for the unfolding of the plot (the movie of life). Remember to Love Everyone and Honor Them for their roles, even those playing the Dark roles or the deep sleeper roles.

Without Energy reflecting all around us and through us, we would never wake up or see deeper parts of ourselves. The deep sleepers have agreed to stay asleep until the 11th hour, and thus they are playing out their roles right until the end. They are teaching us Patience, Compassion, Reflection and Accountability. We are ensuring that we are Healing, Raising our Consciousness enough so that when the deep sleepers do wake up, we are there with open arms to assist them. This is the Divine Balance of this unfoldment.

The more we can remain Non-Attached and remember that the only change we need to focus on is within ourselves, the easier the transition. There are always deeper levels of Understanding and Compassion that we can reach. The more we focus on our Inner Selves, rather than externalizing, the faster we will move up the ladder of Ascension.

However, there is no rush. Being Patient with yourself and your process is key. Everything is part of the Divine Plan and Divine Timing, and the more we Surrender, the grander our journeys will be.

THE PHYSICAL HEALING STAGE

The Physical Healing Stage is the first stage for many; however, as you move through the process, this stage will come up again and again. If this is your starting point, then your focus is on any pain, illness, disease, or ailment your body is currently experiencing. Our bodies take on so much during the Ascension Process, so we have to be very nurturing and patient with our vessels.

Those who are in the Physical Healing Stage will need to focus on this stage first, as the density of the body will not allow for Higher Frequency Energies to be Anchored In until the vessel is cleared.

The first thing you must do is pinpoint the areas of your body which are experiencing pain, illness, or disease. As you now know, every part of the body correlates to one of the Chakras. When a Chakra is damaged or blocked, due to trauma, wounding, or toxins, it creates disease or pain. In order to truly heal, we must identify the Energetic Root cause of the problem.

Once you identify the underlying metaphysical energetics, you can begin to integrate the Emotional Healing Stage. These stages will then run simultaneously.

Here are the **Basic Ascension Tools for Physical Healing** which can be utilized to heal almost every illness or disease:

- ***Swallowing 1 spoonful of coconut oil per day***

- ***Oil Pulling***
  (a spoonful of coconut oil pulled through your teeth, swished around your mouth, and then spit out)

- ***Sprinkling Turmeric Powder on Your Food (or taking it in capsules or infused into tea)***

- ***Doing a Garlic Cleanse*** (1 clove a day for 7 days)

- ***Drinking Quality Water*** (which has been prayed over and blessed)

- ***Sun Gazing***

(During sunrise/sunset, or during the day, spend a minute or two gazing at the sun. If your eyes are particularly sensitive, then you can do this for 10 seconds at a time. This allows the integration of Light Codes into the Third Eye.)

- ***Grounding***
  (Placing your feet on the ground for 20 minutes per day)

- ***Moving for 45 minutes per day***
  (walking, running, dancing, yoga, etc.)

- ***Deep breathing***
  (in through the nose, out through the mouth)

- ***Visualizing the golden, emerald, violet, rainbow flames engulfing and healing your body and brain***

- ***Meditating***

- ***Using Plasma Technology in your home***
  (There are many beings across the planet who are creating and building Plasma Technology. We specifically utilize this technology through Plasma Products such as pyramids, healing wands, and plasma water, which we use for our bodies as well as for plants. Plasma Tech is often used inside pendants and necklaces too.)

- ***Transmuting your food & beverages through intention***
  (Bless your food by Setting the Intention for the food to be filled with Love, Light, and Rainbow Energy, while also intending that all toxins to be transmuted. You can say something like, *"Bless this food to the nourishment of my body"*)

Our bodies are physical healing devices. We are Quantum Technology embodied in physical vessels. Our bodies have the Divine Intelligence of Healing, but it only works at optimal levels for our highest benefit when we are not interfered with by lower vibrations.

Once you begin to understand how your emotions and thoughts affect your physical body, you will begin to experience the effects of Emotional Inner Work and Positive Higher Thoughts. Our bodies are a reflection of our Consciousness. Our Personal Frequency is the biggest source of Healing that we have. If we look at the Vibrational Scale, anything under 200 is a life-draining frequency. This means that if you are in a Vibration under 200, you will be draining your physical life force, causing you to have to take Energy from the external world around you.

At this stage, you should get very familiar with the Vibrational Scale, which will help you identify what Your Average Vibration Per Day is. Life-draining frequencies under 200 include shame, guilt, anger, pride, fear, worry, and arrogance. Dissolving these frequencies will be part of your Emotional Healing Stage, which is often running simultaneously with your Physical Healing Stage.

700
ENLIGHTENMENT
600
PEACE
540
JOY
500
LOVE
5D
400
UNDERSTANDING
350
ACCEPTANS
250
NEUTRALITY
200
COURAGE
4D
175
PRIDE
150
ANGER
100
FEAR
75
GRIEF
50
HOPELESSNESS
30
GUILT
20
SHAME
3D
5DFULLDISCLOSURE.ORG

The other way we assist our bodies in Healing is through our Awareness of what we are putting into them. There are a lot of belief systems in the world about food, alcohol, tobacco, etc., which create more density to the body. In other words, struggling to figure out which system is best for your body creates its own dense and destructive energy in the body. When we attach to one "way" of Healing, or through rigid structures of eating, dieting, working out, etc., we create inner resistance, which only adds to our body's density.

First, organic foods, especially fruits and vegetables, are great for the body. The body can easily absorb these foods and turn them into High Frequency Energy. The more toxic foods we give our body, on the other hand, the more work the body must dedicate to processing it.

If you are struggling with your physical health, you will need to make some lifestyle changes around your food choices to give your body the best chance of purging and releasing density. However, we do NOT advocate diets or belief systems about "bad" food. There is a Divine Balance to it all.

Any and all food, even junk food or fast food, can be transmuted into a higher frequency by Praying Over It with Intention. Do not restrict yourself to any diets or beliefs about what you can and cannot eat. Listen to your body and allow it to have what it is asking for, with no judgement about what that is. Put Intention and Love into the food you eat, which will reverse any negative effects.

That being said, if you are suffering from illness and disease, it's best to focus on purely organic and fresh foods while your body is Healing, later integrating other foods. We also recommend Fasting during the Physical Healing Stage as one of the most beneficial ways to Detox Your Body. If you are new to Fasting, begin with 24 hours and work your way up to 72 hours.

Try and eat organic or fresh foods as much as possible. This includes fruits, vegetables, whole grains, fish, and red meat. Many belief systems perpetuate the thought that meat is "bad" for you and should be cut out of the human diet. This is false. Animals have a specific contract here on Earth to hold the frequencies of Unconditional Love and to provide us food that is essential for our Healing Process. Creation does not make mistakes, and there is a higher purpose for the animals being on Earth. Although lower frequencies such as violence and greed have been dumped into the animals and the production of meat, these will no longer exist in the Ascension Transition. Red meat is essential for the healing of the brain, and it provides necessary enzymes for the body's Healing Process. Eat red meat as you feel guided to and follow the pings of your body.

As you become more attuned to your vessel, it will guide you on what it needs for Healing. If you are craving a certain food, you must discern whether this is your EGO wanting to fill an emotional void with that particular food, or whether your body actually needs it. Focus on how your body feels after you eat that food, which will tell you whether it was an EGO want or the body's need.

Cutting out sugar completely is also a great way to help Heal the body. Sugar is a toxin which destroys the brain and the immune system. Sugar is best only in small doses. (Raw and organic sugar can be used in moderation, once the body has been detoxed from any addiction to artificial sugar.)

Use tools such as coffee and organic tobacco to help keep you grounded in your body during the Ascension Process.

All the belief systems around these tools come from the mind. ANY tool that comes from a natural resource, such as a plant or vegetable, can be used to assist you, if you are Using It with the Right Intention and Blessing the Tool before using it.

The toxins that exist in pharmaceuticals, hard drugs, and imitation food/drinks are poisons to the body. Energy drinks, fake vegan meat, pills, street drugs, vaccines, etc., these are all detrimental to the body. The more of these you have consumed, the more purging your body will need to do; however, the body is very capable of Healing itself, if it is allowed to.

The body craves Nurturing, and the more Self-Care you give yourself, the more your body will respond.

Getting in touch with nature and the elements is also key for your healing. Sun Gazing, Placing Your Feet on the Ground/Grounding, spending moments in Meditation, listening to Music, Stretching, taking Walks, Drinking Water – these are all simple disciplines that show the body Love.

Remember too that our physical bodies are an extension of the body we live on – Planet Earth. The way we treat Earth is a reflection of how we treat ourselves. Focus on your connection to plants, animals, trees, oceans, crystals, etc., allowing natural and organic ways of Healing to occur.

Every natural mineral and element have a purpose, and we are only just beginning to discover the amazing Healing Benefits of all that nature provides us. Spend time doing research and experimenting with different things to see what works best for your body. Each vessel is unique and will tell you what it requires. Be open to trying anything that resonates for you, whether this be Visualizing Healing Meditations, Herbal and Holistic Healing Tools, Breathing and Movement Healing such as Yoga/Qi Gong, or trying Physical Healing Tools such as Plasma, Crystals, or Animal Therapy.

Remember that all belief systems about the body are not true. The human mind can never truly understand the workings of the human vessel because the human vessel is a Quantum Body run on Divine Intelligence. The mind can only understand things based on the past, or things that have a black and white answer. The body will never fit into a black and white model. Therefore, most of the "medicine" we currently have in our medical field is based on the past, and on a very limited understanding of the body.

We can see how this manifests in the pharmaceutical industry. This industry was literally created to keep bodies sick so that the medical industry could financially boom. Healed people don't make the system money. Doctors and hospitals ruthlessly push these medications, and many of them truly think they are beneficial and that they work. If doctors truly understood Energy and the Divine Intelligence of the body, they would never recommend pharmaceuticals as a solution.

Taking Back the Power of Your Own Healing is key to Taking Back Your Sovereignty. You have to know and feel that you are a Powerful Healer, that your body is a Natural Healer, and that you have the ability to cure yourself of anything.

Since all illness and disease are based on Energy, as you Heal yourself, you also help Heal the Collective Energy, as well as your family DNA line, who carry the same energetic density you do.

THE EMOTIONAL HEALING STAGE

The Emotional Healing Stage will often run simultaneously throughout your process, always coming back around in layers. Our Emotional Bodies are so damaged from trauma, wounding, and programming. Most of us were never taught how to process our emotions, how to let them go, and how to Heal them. Since childhood, we have essentially been stuffing down our emotions or clinging and attaching to them.

All pain, illness, and disease has an emotional component. Many of the lower emotions that affect our body can be inherited through the DNA, which is why infants can be born with things like asthma, cancer, autism, etc. These are a mix of emotional traumas that are inherited and/or toxins that are passed from mother to child.

Working through our Emotional Bodies and Clearing Out Density is a very intense process. For most of us, we feel very overwhelmed at the depth of emotional pain we are actually holding. The key with this stage is to not take anything personally, and to be Non-Attached.

We must remember that all of those who have "hurt" us were playing a role for us to Wake Up, Heal our Wounds, and to Take on Transformation for the Collective. All lower emotions stem from us taking this personally and being attached to who we think we are (known as our identity construct). Many have experienced abuse, neglect, abandonment, betrayal, or judgment. We internalize these experiences and in turn experience anger, resentment, guilt, shame, and self-hatred.

Understand that you as a soul committed to come here to Earth, many times, in order to Heal Collective Karma. You can then begin to see life as one big drama playing out for us to see. All of Humanity is wounded, thus we recreate wounds, and we instill wounds in our children. There is no blame, no judgment, or punishment for this. However, there is the Responsibility to Heal as our part of the Ascension Process.

The biggest challenge within this phase is Unpacking All the Layers of Trauma and Wounding We Hold. Most of this will stem from childhood, and you will see how these wounds and fears re-created themselves in your later life experiences. Most children develop their Emotional Bodies around the ages of 7 to 14. (This is when children and teenagers become "over emotional", reclusive, angry, rebellious, etc. It is because their Emotional Body is beginning to show the trauma and wounds, both from their DNA and their childhood experiences.) They are not taught how to Express Their Feelings about their traumas and wounds, Process them, or Heal them, so it all gets stored in their Emotional Body.

It is not until we Consciously Choose to Unravel These Wounds that they begin to Release. Most beings avoid this their entire life because the pain and depth of the emotions are often too much to handle. This comes from judgement. There is an ancestral fear within us about looking at our pain. It means we have to Feel Those Feelings of anger, guilt, and shame, and we do not wish to feel that. That is why most beings never make it through the Healing Process. Once they get to the painful part, they either shut down or quit.

Our lack of feeling has been cut off, so we aren't able to access our Emotional Bodies anymore. In an effort to fill this void of the lack of feeling, we try and use external things, like possessions, money, relationships, food, drugs, or sex.

The other scenario that holds us back is when we do begin moving through the traumas and the wounds, but we have attached so deeply to them, we hold onto them. Some people spend years in therapy and never really grow. Why? Because they are continuing to think, analyze, and focus on their traumas in a never-ending loop. They aren't looking at them as just experiences their soul chose to have and then let go of. Instead, they create storylines and attach to the human drama of it all. At the surface level, there is always a story, but on the Energetic Level, it's simply an Energy that has come to you to Transform.

The biggest challenge during the Emotional Healing Stage is to stick with it. Once the wound is triggered, you are going to feel pain and uncomfortable emotions. When you hit this point, remember to use the Healing Tools – Deep Breathing, Cutting Out All Thought, Being Non-Attached to the Emotion, Not Taking It Personally, Extending Forgiveness (to yourself, to all others, and to the experience itself),

Expressing Yourself (cry, scream, break something (safely)). Whatever you need to do to Let It Out and Transform It … do that. There is no judgement on how we go through this process.

During this stage, your greatest gifts will be *re-hearting* that *"NOTHING is personal …EVERYTHING is simply ENERGY"*. We are all vessels contracted to take on certain experiences, certain triggers, and certain programming to transform for the Collective. Dig deep within yourself to find your deepest levels of Compassion and Forgiveness for those who have hurt you … because they too are hurt. (Forgiveness Ceremonies are very powerful and a great tool to utilize. By writing down everything – and everyone – you wish to forgive and then burning your list, you agree to let go of the Energy. This is how you end a Karmic Cycle.)

Grief is another deep emotion that will come up for Release. Moving through the 7 Stages of Grief (Disbelief/Shock, Denial, Guilt and Pain, Bargaining, Anger, Depression, and Acceptance), you can see where you still have any anger, despair, depression, etc. and Accept Those Emotions. The more we try and change how we feel or "get out of it", the more in resistance we are. Sometimes, just Accepting the Emotions We're Feeling, and where we are in our healing, takes off the pressure and relieves the judgment of ourselves, Allowing the Energy to Release.

Journaling and Automatic Writing are great tools during this stage. Writing down everything and anything that is coming to you will help you process your thoughts and feelings. Focusing on Inner Stillness through this process (perhaps by utilizing Meditation), will help bring a Deep Sense of Peace within your being. If you struggle to sit still and constantly find yourself distracted, this is a sign that your Emotional Body is extremely damaged. The mind does not want you to sit still because, as soon as you are still, not distracted and not in thought, the buried emotions begin to surface, which makes you feel fidgety and uncomfortable. Keep practicing Stillness, and you will find amazing Healing within it.

Tools for Emotional Healing:

- ***Candles, room sprays, incense, and sage***
- ***Working with crystals***
- ***Journaling***
- ***Doing things that bring you joy and peace***
- ***Stillness and meditation***
- ***Deep breathing***
- ***Listening to music***
- ***Creating art***
- ***Nurturing your body with foods that bring you joy***
- ***Water therapy (showers, pools, oceans, etc.)***
- ***Using sacred tools for processing (such as marijuana or alcohol)***

➤ ***Accessing your inner child and focusing on play/creating***

THE MENTAL HEALING STAGE

For many, this stage occurs after the Physical and Emotional Healing have begun; however, if the mind and/or mental illness is a struggle for you, then this may be one of your first stages. If you have a damaged Mental Body, you will experience anxiety, depression, fears, paranoia, thought loops, and lower perceptions. If you experience frequent headaches, migraines, eye pressure, anxiety in the body, then the Mental Body is stressed and filled with density.

Due to how deeply we are in the EGO mind and how programmed we have become to attach to our thoughts, the Mental Healing Stage can be challenging. In this stage, what we are de-programming is the lower thought system. Lower thoughts are any thought that does not bring us Joy or Inspiration. During this phase, your focus is on understanding EGO-Programming and how it affects your thoughts and actions.

The basis of the EGO is belief systems. Belief systems are illusionary thoughts that we believe are true, but they are not true, and thus we create a construct and perspective of the world through the lens of these belief systems. All lower thoughts stem from fear. Fear is the root of all pain and suffering, and it comes through each and every programming.

When we are in the mind, and our Mental Body is fragmented, damaged, or blocked, it creates distorted thoughts and perceptions. These manifest as judgements, opinions, belief systems, assumptions, and mental anxiety. We can see the manifestation of this within the Collective as rising levels of mental illness. Mental illness is nothing more than a severely damaged or imbalanced Mental Body, and truly, all Humanity is mentally ill because we are all in our minds.

The brain and the mind are two separate things. The brain is an organ and plays a critical role in Divine Intelligence, Intuition, and Creative Inspiration. The mind, however, is a program, similar to a virus running on your computer, which hijacks and takes over the brain's functions. The Dark wanted to ensure that all Humanity was mentally ill, which is also why we have been poisoned through our water, air, food, medicine, and drugs, all to further damage the brain and ensure that it is never fully-functioning.

When you begin to dissolve the mind's programming, your brain begins to activate its dormant parts, specifically the right brain. The right brain is our connection to Source, our Divine Intuition, Divine Intelligence, and God-Consciousness (the feminine aspect of the brain). The left brain is the masculine aspect which was hijacked by the mind and keeps us in logic, analytics, and reasoning. These on their own are not "bad", but without balance, they are extremely destructive.

What has occurred is that the left brain is the only side truly functioning, as most of the right brain is not activated. This is why we have split hemispheres of the brain. The Dark manipulated our DNA to sever the brain. In 5D, however, we will have 100% usage of our full brain.

We overanalyze and rely so heavily on our masculine logic and reasoning, we can only see things in black and white, right and wrong, good or bad. In Truth, nothing in the Universe exists in duality. On Earth, however, and only on Earth, because we have manifested a black and white reality for ourselves using our free will, our minds categorize and analyze everything within that duality.

As soon as we judge something as "good" or "bad" or "right" or "wrong", we are in the mind. A clear Mental Body holds no judgement and no opinions because it knows that All Wisdom Lies in the Heart. It sees the higher perspective – that everything exists to show us something … that everything is part of the Divine Plan. The healed Mental Body allows in only Divine thoughts, not lower thoughts, and thus begins to create a different reality.

In order to heal the Mental Body, use the following mantra:

"I don't know shit."

This will help delete thoughts that convince you something is true that is not true. Another tool is Cutting Cords – as soon as you begin having lower thoughts, cut the proverbial cord to those thoughts, and replace them with higher thoughts, such as *"I am Divine"*, *"I am Love"*, *"I am Worthy."*

During this phase, it's important to be very disciplined with your Spiritual Tools.

The following tools are vital for this stage:

- ***Cutting Cords with all negative thoughts***
  "I cut cords with everyone and everything and all events; I re-attach all my energetic cords to everything whole, pure, true, and in resonance with Love."

- ***Use Mirror Affirmations everyday using 20 of your favorite "I AM" Affirmations***

- ***Meditate and Practice Stillness (without thoughts)***

- ***Make No Assumptions***

- ***See the Higher Perspective (in all things)***

- ***Focus on Activating the Right Brain and Visualizing the Reconnection of the Left***

and Right Brain Hemispheres, as well as Visualizing Rainbow Energy Lighting Up and Healing All Brain Synapses

- ***Ask Your Angels for Confirms and Synchronicities on What is True***

THE SPIRITUAL HEALING STAGE

This stage often occurs last, or it will come in once the Mental Body has been Healed. The reason is that if the Mental Body is damaged, or a being is still heavily in the mind, they cannot connect to their hearts and feel the Truths of Higher Consciousness. If you attempt to understand and comprehend Spirituality and Energy when your Mental Body is still unhealed, it will result in Spiritual or Super EGO.

The biggest blocks to Spiritual Healing are religious belief systems and our deep wound of separation from God/the Divine Mother. All humans have the separation from Source wound to Heal because we enter into physicality with amnesia. We forget we are fractals of Source. We then are ingrained with religious belief systems.

The Dark, for example, purposely flipped the concept of the true God, which is Mother of All Creation. Source is a feminine essence, as the feminine energy creates and births things into existence. Father of All Creation, the masculine part of God, is the structure for the feminine creator energy. The masculine are the containers and manifesters of the Source energy.

The Dark then went further and created an external, masculine God (a God outside of us). That was done because masculine (yang energy) represents the external manifestation of an energy. Thus, the image of God was always missing its feminine aspect, the Mother, the bringer of life. Their image of God was empty. It had no Spirit in it. It was just a container, an image. And this created a deep distortion within our Spiritual Bodies, as all of us are craving our connection back with God. Many claimed to have found that connection within religion and the connection to a masculine God, yet they have deep spiritual wounds and are still holding onto a lot of rules, regulations, belief systems, and judgements. They are missing the feminine piece.

During this phase, it's about Letting Go of Everything You Think You Know about God and then Connecting with the Mother aspect/Mother God. If this triggers something within you, reflect on what Mother/Feminine wounds you have or the suppression of your own Inner Feminine. Feel into how this opens up your connection to Source and sparks you to Heal Your Wound of Separation from God. This is how we bring in Balanced Harmonics.

The other part of the Spiritual Healing Stage is reflecting on how you are out of balance internally. Masculine beings are meant to be 51% masculine and 49% feminine, while feminine beings are 51% feminine and 49% masculine.

Look at the following Divine Traits and see which ones you are lacking:

Divine Feminine Traits/Aspects:

Receiving
Intuition
Compassion
Receptivity
Responding

Divine Masculine Traits/Aspects:

Courage
Integrity
Discipline
Action

Focus on strengthening the aspects that you have not fully integrated, allowing, embracing, and taking inspired actions so that you can come into greater inner balance.

It's often during this stage too that you will begin to understand what your role and purpose is here on Earth. You may begin to get Downloads and a Greater Connection to Your Angels (through Synchronicities and Messages). This is the Higher Self activating.

Automatic Writing will be your greatest tool. You simply sit down, with no preconceived thoughts, and you ask your Angels and Higher Self to please share with you any wisdom or information. Without second-guessing yourself or doubting what is coming through, you write down anything that comes to you, trusting that whatever is coming in is meant for you. You can also connect with Source/Mother during these moments and ask for her to share with you.

Spiritual Disciplines are essential during this phase as well. When the Spiritual Body begins to Heal, you will begin to Start Integrating Your Lost Soul Fragments. You may have flashbacks of past lives or feel that a certain essence is coming to you to embody.

To avoid Spiritual EGO, simply write down whatever is coming to you and then let it go. If the idea or thought comes back to you 3x, or you receive 3 confirms, then you know it's real. It's important during this process that we do not attach to the past or to who we think we are. All that's important is that it's giving back to us a piece of ourselves to integrate.

The greatest hijack that occurs during the Spiritual Healing Stage is Lightworker Syndrome. This is the belief that now that you have accessed higher levels of consciousness and may have some new gifts and insights coming to you, that you are above others or know more than others. Always remember that everyone is playing a role, and our evolution is never ending.

The completion of this stage never ends. We are constantly coming to New Awareness, and new pieces of information resonate with us. Do not hold onto or attach to any information that comes to you.

You may feel guided to begin shifting into your role of service to others. This is the path to Full Spiritual Healing, which is to be in service to the greater good. Get in touch with what really brings you Joy and with the Gifts that you are and can offer, and then Share those with the world. At the same time, Detach from needing validation or external guidance and Commit to Following Your Heart and Trusting Your Intuition.

As you develop a closer relationship with Source and your Higher Self, you will begin to be guided onto the next steps of your path. This is where things can once more get uncomfortable. The Lightworker Syndrome convinces many that they can have the Spiritual Path while also having the comfortable path. This is not true. Spiritual Healing is all about stepping into Love and the Unknown, the only two energies in existence.

Part of Healing is to fully Anchor In Trust for Yourself, Source, and the Divine Plan. You may be guided to leave your job, family, relationship, living situation, etc. in order to step into a higher place of growth. This isn't always the case, but you will know if it applies to you because you will begin feeling as if nothing resonates with you in the now, and you will feel the urge to follow your heart into your next phase.

As we work through these various stages of Healing and Integration, we learn Patience, Self-Reflection, Accountability, Forgiveness and Compassion … for ourselves and others. These stages cannot be rushed, and we cannot compare our journey to anyone else's! We are all unique, so these stages will look different for each of us. The most important thing is that we are learning to reconnect with ourselves, our bodies, our emotions, and our spiritual connections.

This allows us to feel grounded in our physical experience and to no longer be seeking distractions, escapes, or reaction states. Once we have fully surrendered and opened ourselves up to this process and have allowed our bodies to begin Healing, we then move into the real spiritual work – the dissolving of our EGO-programmed minds.

Through Awareness, Accountability, Acceptance and Inspired Action, we dissolve the Old Programmings that keep us in lower states of existence. It's often a challenging process, but it is also beautiful, transformational, and truly soul-opening to do this work. As we each take on our individual pieces of transformation, we assist all Humanity in its transformation. We are truly doing this as ONE.

CHAPTER TWENTY-ONE: BREAKING THROUGH THE EGO

In order to begin dissolving the EGO Mind, you must first become Aware of it. The EGO stays alive and thrives through your lack of awareness, or ignorance, of it. To deny you have EGO, or to be ignorant of its Programmings, is to give it power. Once we become aware of a Programming, the Programming can no longer function. Through consistent Self-Awareness, we eventually come to dissolve our Programmings and operate at a Higher Dimensional Level. This is not to say that you will never experience EGO again … far from it.

Once you begin dissolving your EGO and begin reaching higher levels of Consciousness, the EGO can sense its own death, and it seeks to fight to maintain power. *Sound familiar?* This is the tactic that the Cabal has used to cling to power, at all costs. It is the ONLY thing the EGO knows how to do because it cannot Surrender, it cannot Let Go. As you move up the Consciousness Scale, your EGO will fight back. However, once it has lost its power, thanks to the tools and techniques I'm sharing with you, it is quickly and easily transformed.

It is important to understand and realize that many of you will have, what we call, "Core Programmings." These are your main Programmings which are deeply ingrained in your DNA through ancestral karma. These Programs have been passed down to you, and they are the hardest to transform. They require Full Accountability and Honesty with Yourself.

When we are first transforming these Core Programs, we often have an attachment to their energetics, as they are the most familiar to us. This will manifest for us as an external attachment or behavior pattern that is difficult to break. For example, if one has a Deep Programming of Victim Consciousness, they will want to cling to others who overpower them or cling to a sense of external authority to save them. At their core, they are afraid to take Accountability for themselves and thus, they repeat patterns of victim/savior, blame and abuse.

True Dedication and Heart Willingness are required to get through and beyond these Core Programmings.

Once you have finished learning about each of these Core Programs (as detailed throughout this chapter), sit with yourself and be truly honest about your own Core Programs. Once you have identified them, you must cut the cords of your attachment to them and their corresponding habits and behaviors. You must go cold turkey with these attachments, the reason being that, until the attachments themselves and habits are broken, the energetic of the Program will not be transformed. Eventually, after you have mastered the attachments, you will then be able to Come into Balance with these habits, behaviors, or external things/persons.

It is very comparable to someone who struggles with addiction. Every human being is an energy addict. We each just express our addiction in different forms. The greatest addictions of energy are to control dramas, sex, food, sleep, drugs, shopping, relationships, and validation.

In order to heal any energy addiction, you must first be "sober" when it comes to the particular behaviors associated with the addiction. That said, the label of "addict" has become a much-used crutch.

Those in 3D who suffer with alcohol or drug addiction, for example, convince themselves that they have to be totally "sober" for the rest of their lives, believing that the addiction is so overpowering to them that they cannot engage in the behavior, at all, without spiraling out of control, which means that they can never really Heal the Underlying Energy of their addiction. Once Healed, however, and that level of Healing is possible, the lower energy addiction would no longer even be there. Thus, the former addict would be able to neutrally engage in that behavior or action.

When dealing with the EGO, we must take a "sober" period from our attachments, meaning we no longer allow them to have power over us. We are not victims, nor are we under the control of our EGOs and attachments. We are able to Master Our Energy and once again Come into Balance with the things we Love, but in a purified state.

Once you have identified your attachments and Core Programs, commit yourself to going 30 days cold turkey from that attachment. Use the tools and techniques outlined in this book to Keep Aligning, Transforming, Processing and Expanding. After 30 days, work with yourself on Coming into Balance with these behaviors or things/people. Continue in a trial-and-error process of correcting and adjusting as you become more and more Self-Aware and Self-Correcting.

THE EGO PROGRAMMINGS

LACK OF WISDOM

Lack of Wisdom can appear in two ways: it can come from a lack of experience or a lack of growing from experiences. Wisdom is gained through seeing *the lesson and the blessing* within every experience. When one does NOT learn the lesson of the experience, they repeat the lesson, over and over again. These beings are embodying Lack of Wisdom Programming. They lack the awareness and personal accountability to fully see their role in manifesting their experiences.

Most with this Programming will be in denial that they have it. That's the nature of Lack of Wisdom Programming. It always thinks it knows something when it really doesn't. The easiest way to know if you have this is: if you are afraid to say you don't know something, if you always have to have a response to everything, or if you have repeated lessons that continue to appear in your life in different forms.

If this is a Core Programming for you, you must look at where you are repeating patterns that are creating pain and suffering. This could be through repeating toxic relationship patterns, repeating lower behaviors that continue to manifest lower experiences for you, or any other situation or experience that repeats itself because you have not mastered the lesson of it.

To transform this Core EGO-Programming requires Self-Reflecting, Taking Accountability, Mastering the Lessons of the Experiences, and Choosing to Stop the Repeating Loops.

LACK OF EXPERIENCE

This ties in with Lack of Wisdom but also presents itself by its resistance to change. The EGO does not like new experiences, as the unknown makes it uncomfortable. Now, you may be someone who thinks, "I love new experiences. I love traveling and trying new foods and meeting new people." This is a good sign that you are indeed open to new things, however, you must also look at the areas in your life in which you have resisted change or new opportunities. This will typically come in as a resistance to doing something we don't like (or "think" we do not like) or something that our EGO does not want to do.

For example, it is easy for one to be open to traveling to new places or experiencing new people and environments, but that same being might have resistance to learning how to sew, trying a sport they've never tried, or camping in the cold. We often embrace new experiences that align with what we "think" we like and want, meaning whatever our preferences are. However, we usually resist new experiences that go against what our EGOs want, need and desire. We are open ONLY to some new experiences, if they meet our wants, but we are not open to ALL experiences.

If this is one of your Core Programs, you will see a pattern within your life where you have often remained comfortable. You didn't go outside the box or try new things. You didn't take leaps of faith or take on any challenges. You played it safe.

In this case, you must Start Saying YES! to Life. Feel into what you have the MOST resistance to doing and do that thing. Say YES! to new opportunities or things you wouldn't normally say yes to. This breaks the Programming, opening you up to things that help you grow.

LACK OF COMPASSION

This is a very common Programming for a masculine or feminine being who has an overabundance of masculine energy. Lack of Compassion comes from the root of judgment. When we judge others, we make an assumption about them, perceiving them from our own lenses of experience. This creates a separation between you and that person, leading to a Lack of Compassion for that soul and their journey.

If you struggle to find compassion for others, or find you are overly critical of others, cold and detached, then you have to heal your own lack of feeling. The reason we blame and judge others is because we can't feel them. If we could truly feel ourselves, we would then fully feel others as being one with us. To judge another or be harsh or cold to another is to do the same to yourself.

If this is one of your Core Programmings, your focus must be on Learning to Feel. Once per day, focus on deep breathing. Breathe in Love through your nose and out your mouth. Feel the breath permeating your entire vessel and then imagine Love flowing back out into your environment. If you can focus on your breath and your body for just a few minutes per day, you will Establish a Conscious Connection with Your Body. This begins to Open Up Your Feeling Centers.

Also focus on where you lack Self-Love. Wherever you judge, criticize, or are hard on yourself, that is where you will find your Lack of Compassion. Everything begins with us, WITHIN US. However we treat ourselves is how we treat others. Find your Self-Compassion first and Fully Accept Yourself as you are.

LACK OF PASSION

Where Lack of Compassion is the lack of feminine energy within a being, Lack of Passion is the lack of masculine energy. This can come through a feminine or overly feminine masculine. Passion is a Divine Trait – the fire and Divine Will of Source. Passion is untamed and often gets perceived as anger, yet the frequencies are entirely different. Anger is based on resentment, blame, and judgment. Passion is based on Honor, Integrity, and Inspiration.

Organically, we are all full of Passion! We are Inspired, Excited, Motivated, and Dedicated Beings. We are Galactic Souls. However, we may have lost some of that Passion while in our physical vessel because the 3D realm can be so dense to navigate. There is control, authority, power over, and manipulation in the 3D realm. The key is to not allow those things to extinguish your fire. Remember that, you are more powerful than anything outside of yourself.

If this your Core Program, you must Get Back in Touch with Your Inner Fire. Passion is Inspiration in Action. This can come through speech or creativity expressed with vigor! Look within at where you are afraid of your own power, and there you will find your Lack of Passion. *When did you give your power away? What is stopping you from taking back your power?*

Use whatever tools help motivate you into action. This can be music, listening to motivational speeches, physical movement, or verbal expression (and yes … that can include yelling 😉).

LACK OF PERCEPTION

As humans using our minds, we only perceive 5-6% of all energies in existence. The density of our bodies as well as our limiting belief systems prevent us from perceiving other energies. In our 3D body, we have been limited to 5 senses. Our "6th sense" (or Intuition) only begins to develop as our Consciousness expands through Inner Work and Experiences.

Lack of Perception appears when one is very limited in their scope of understanding, based on limiting belief systems, lack of intuition, and lack of experience. This prevents a being from having a higher perspective – one who does not see things as good/bad/right/wrong. If you lack perception, it is because you are making judgments, assumptions, or opinions when you are unable to understand all the energy at play.

To transform this energy, we must Re-Heart Ourselves that We Know Nothing. When we know nothing, we know everything! Only an empty vessel, one without an EGO lens, can truly access full perception and cosmic wisdom.

A great practice to transform this energy is Repeating the Mantra, *"I don't know shit,"* and then Consciously Letting Go of What You Think You Know.

If this is a Core Program for you, you must Cut Cords with all your opinions and judgments. Catch yourself as soon as you begin to have a lower thought about another person, an experience, or situation. Say out loud, *"I don't know shit"*, then come to a place of feeling into this person or situation rather than looking at the surface-level story. Realize that everyone is acting from a place of their own wounding, and the experiences that happen are always for our highest growth. Not everything needs a label or an explanation. Focus on the Higher in all people and experiences, and there, you will find Divine Perception.

LACK OF INTEGRITY

This is a huge energetic for Humanity – both internal and external. Externally, Lack of Integrity will present itself as someone who cannot follow through on tasks, someone who says they are going to do something and doesn't do it. These are beings who are not in integrity with their words or actions, either consciously or unconsciously.

Internally, Lack of Integrity presents itself when we fail to honor ourselves and what is highest and best for us. There are thoughts, emotions, behavioral patterns, and dynamics we know do not serve us, yet we stay in or with them because we lack integrity with ourselves. We fail to keep ourselves accountable, and we allow ourselves to make inner compromises that slowly deteriorate our soul.

If this is a Core Programming for you, your biggest challenge is going to be Self-Accountability. To transform this energetic, you must Focus on Following Through – finishing a task from beginning to end and making sure that anything you tell yourself or say out loud that you are going to do, you do. This keeps you in Full Integrity, both within and without.

Discernment is a key Divine Trait to utilize when transforming this Programming. We often commit to things or say we will do something simply out of obligation, guilt or trying to people please others. Then, we cannot follow through on our commitment because we were never aligned with it. Each moment, Discern What is Actually Best for You as a soul, what will help you grow and expand, and only Commit to Those Things.

LACK OF HONOR

Lack of Honor is the brother of Lack of Integrity. When we lack honor, we do not value ourselves nor do we value others or life itself. Honor comes from the knowing that we are one with all and that everything in existence has the Spark of Source within it (except for those things created by the Dark, without souls). Lack of Honor comes from the deep belief system of being separate.

This Programming plays out in numerous ways. One way is that we do not treat ourselves with honor. We do not care for ourselves, nurture ourselves, or take accountability for ourselves. We make excuses and justifications for our behavior, often focusing on external excuses rather than our internal choices. Two, we do not treat others and everything in the world with honor. There are many examples of this, such as a disregard for others and their feelings, a disregard for the Earth, and a lack of care of and for things that may or may not be priorities in our lives.

To transform this, we must Return to the Sacredness of All Life. We must feel and remember how amazing it is for everything to be in existence, to See All Things as Part of Source, and have respect for that. This includes the people in our lives, ourselves, and the things we have. When we Honor each and every being, animal, item and environment, we also Honor Ourselves.

If this is your Core Programming, there is a lack of feeling involved. You must Focus on Developing Your Own Self-Worth as well as Seeing the Higher Aspects and the Beauty within Others and All Things.

LACK OF EMPATHY

Lack of Empathy often gets confused with Lack of Compassion. Compassion is the ability to Hold Space for another – for where they are in their journey or for yourself in exactly where you are. Empathy involves the ability to truly feel what another is feeling. This requires the Opening of Your Heart and your Ability to be Vulnerable.

When we lack empathy, we have a block in our hearts from being able to feel what another is feeling. You are unable to share a connection with that being's experience. Even if we cannot live in that other being's experience, we can resonate with the underlying emotional wound and meet them there.

To transform this Programming, it requires working with Opening your Heart Chakra, first being able to Feel Your own Emotions, Your own Wounding, Your own Traumas and Vulnerabilities. Most humans have stuffed down or locked away many parts of themselves in an effort to stay "safe" from experiencing pain. This actually stores the trauma within the body, and the body becomes sick.

If this is one of your Core Programmings, Focus on Your Breath. Breathing deeply and consciously in through the nose and out through the mouth, for a few minutes each day, you begin to Ignite the Feeling Centers and Open Up Your Heart Portal. You begin to Be In Tune With your body, your emotions, and any pain that you have stored. Through breathing and Focusing on the Frequency of Love, you begin to Heal these parts of you, while also being able to Feel More Deeply and Allow Yourself to be Vulnerable.

LACK OF FEELING

Lack of Feeling is one of the most wide-spread Programmings amongst the Collective. We have been taught to cut off our feelings and operate solely from the mind (through thought). We are also disconnected from our Emotional Bodies and feelings. Society today is made up solely of distractions, stress, and fight-or-flight. We are unable to be still, or at least, way out of practice of being still.

Lack of Feeling causes many dysfunctions, especially in relationships. Those who are able to feel deeply often feel they are going insane because those around them cannot understand why they are so “emotional”. The challenge with this is that all energy must be expressed, whether consciously or unconsciously. Those who are cut off from their feeling centers are not able to process their emotions, and therefore, they unconsciously express the lower emotional frequencies – such as anger, fear, and revenge. This greatly affects those in their direct environments. In addition, the lower frequencies get dumped into the Collective Consciousness. Those who feel energies strongly are then disproportionately affected by this and must process more for those who are not processing on their own.

Because we do not like to feel pain, we instead choose to feel nothing. This cuts us off from actually Healing and being able to feel things like Unconditional Love, Bliss, and true Joy. To transform Lack of Feeling requires Patience and Practice. Deep Breathing also allows for increased feeling, as does Stillness.

If this is one of your Core Programs, you have to Focus on Being Still. For many of you, this is quite the challenge. For others, you may be able to be still externally but have no ability to be internally still.

Practice being completely still, cutting cords with all thoughts, and just feeling and Being Completely Immersed in the Present Moment of Now. This will take practice, again and again … and again. Finally, you will become still enough to feel all the emotions that need to come up. Allow these to be expressed and processed and use your Spiritual Disciplines to do the Healing work.

LACK OF SELF-LOVE

We cannot truly Love others because we truly do not Love ourselves. Many people "think" they have Self-Love, but it is actually vanity, self-obsession, or externalization. Self-Love is shown by Discipline, Integrity, Honor and the Nurturing of One's Spirit. Humanity has confused Self-Love with the worshipping of the body, while completely forgetting about the Self-Care of the Soul.

This is apparent through our lack of tolerance for others or certain experiences. We are so reactive as a Collective, we cannot Love others unconditionally. This is all stems from being unable to Love ourselves unconditionally. Those who lack Self-Love will typically also have the Core Programs of co-dependency, lack of integrity, lack of honor, unworthiness, vanity, lack of self-care, victim consciousness, and projection.

To heal this, Focus on Nurturing Your Soul rather than your physical body and your needs, wants and desires. The soul requires Stillness, Breath Work, Spiritual Disciplines, Healing and also Passion. When we Love ourselves, we strive to be our grandest selves because we Love US! When we Love ourselves, it is easy to Love others unconditionally because you see them as part of you.

If this is one of your Core Programmings, Focus on Getting In Tune with Your Higher Self. Spend time with your Higher Self and begin to see and focus on all the brilliant aspects of your soul. See the beauty within yourself and remember that you are part of Source, made in perfection. Write a Love Letter to yourself, do your Spiritual Disciplines, Take Care of Your Physical Vessel, and Do the Things that Make You Feel Fulfilled.

UNWORTHINESS

Unworthiness lies within all of us and will be one of the Core Programmings for each being. This Programming was instilled so deeply in order to keep us enslaved to the 3D system, believing that we are not worthy of more. It is the mindset that we should be happy with what we have, never striving for greater, allowing things into our lives which are not good for us but have been made "normal".

This presents itself in many ways:

- Working at jobs we don't like because we do not feel that we are good enough for a grander role.
- Staying in relationships that do not fulfill us out of fear that there is nothing better for us or that we don't deserve better.
- Keeping ourselves small and our dreams small because we do not feel capable or deserving of a better life. We play it safe, we stay in line, and we stay comfortable.

Transforming unworthiness is a long process. The greatest tests during our transformation are confusing worthiness with entitlement. We are Worthy of Unconditional Love, Joy, and Abundance. These are our birthrights as souls. However, we are not entitled to what we think this looks like, especially if we are not embodying these things. For example, if you feel you are worthy of a better relationship, reflect on whether or not YOU are being the greatest version of yourself and being the best partner you can be. As another example, you are worthy of abundance, but are you entitled to it if you do not actually put in any work or dedication?

Entitlement comes from laziness. It is an unequal energy exchange. You want something but are not willing to give anything in return. Becoming worthy means realizing that you are both worthy of receiving grandness, but also being grand and giving grandness. This is true worthiness.

If this is your Core Programming, Look at the Places in Your Life Where You Have Made Yourself Small, where you have Accepted Less Than What You Have Earned, and also look at the Areas in which You are Expecting Something But Have Not Given Yourself.

IGNORANCE

Ignorance means lack of awareness. This comes from ignoring Love … because Love is Awareness. It is Consciousness. Unconsciousness is ignoring or denying the frequencies of Love. It is to stay in the Dark rather than step into the Light. This is the battle between the heart and the mind. The heart is always seeking to Love more, grow more, and gain more Awareness. The mind on the other hand seeks to take, to stay comfortable and safe, and to stay ignorant of Truths that make it uncomfortable.

The good news is that this Programming typically dissolves the moment we Awaken to a higher Truth. The moment we become Aware that there is something more going on than what meets the eye, we begin searching for the Truth. This is the moment when the ignorance dies as we are beginning to seek the Truth rather than run from it.

The greatest test to re-program this tendency is to be able to Hold Space and Compassion for Those Still Choosing Ignorance. This takes Patience and a high level of Non-Attachment to Others and their journey, so that we do not seek to force them into Awakening. They must choose it themselves.

ARROGANCE

Arrogance lies at a Vibration of 190, just below 200, which is the threshold where you move from life-draining frequencies into Life-Enhancing Frequencies. There is a very thin line between arrogance, pride, and courage.

Arrogance comes from a wound of unworthiness, where a being feels the need to place themselves above another or create the façade of greatness when only weakness lies beneath. Arrogance comes from a deeply wounded child.

The positive aspect is that it is not far off from being able to be flipped to the higher vibration of Courage. To transform arrogance into Courage, we must Drop the Façade. We must be able to Humble Ourselves and realize we are above no other, yet we can Inspire others through our Passion and Courage, rather than seeking to put ourselves on a pedestal. Inner Child Healing is essential for this process.

If this is one of your Core Programs, dive into how you felt as a child and where you are holding onto any childhood wounding, such as separation, abandonment, neglect, abuse, repression, or guilt. Through Forgiveness and Self-Love, you come to the place of Knowing Your Brilliance, but also Acknowledging the Higher in Others as well.

ATTACHMENT

Attachment presents itself in obvious as well as more subtle ways. It can manifest as a deep co-dependency in relationships, a need for validation from friends and family, or making choices based on the expectations of others. This can also present as a fear of new experiences, wanting to stay in the same place on the same schedule or same routine. Finally, it can present as a reliance on possessions or constantly seeking to buy and consume to fill an inner void. It's being unable to let things (or people or places) go.

Many beings don't believe they have attachments, yet they unconsciously cling to things. They may also jump from one thing to the next, and then to the next. They may not be attached to a single person/thing/place, but they have an attachment energy that always needs something to hold onto, no matter what or who it is.

To transform attachment, we must Anchor In Acceptance. Once we realize that we are all on our own unique journeys, we realize that we cannot control anyone else's experience. We can only make choices based on what is highest for ourselves. To do this, we can no longer view things in the same way society taught us. We don't always choose lower experiences just because we are afraid of the unknown or of a new experience. We do so because that's what we've been taught to do. Instead, we must Welcome Change and Trust Our Own Journey.

If this is one of your Core Programs, you must learn to Let Go. Control will be your biggest challenge to overcome as you realize how much you cling to the external or your ability to control your environment. If you are attached to people, you must learn to Give Others Space, to let them make their own choices, and to not take their choices or actions personally. Stop changing yourself to meet the needs of others. If you are attached to places, you may need to feel into whether or not you have resisted change and a new environment out of the need for familiarity. If you are attached to things, cleaning your space and letting old things go makes way for new things to come in. You may also need to refrain from excess buying and consuming.

TAKING ENERGY

Energy is the greatest addiction on the planet, and all human minds have this addiction. Because we have lived in the 3D realm, which is based on fear, pain and suffering, we exist in a constant state of fight or flight. This keeps our vibration below 200, which are all the life-draining frequencies. This means that 95% of human beings are constantly in a life-draining state and must take energy from the external in order to sustain themselves. When we exist at Life-

Enhancing Frequencies, which is anything above 250, we then have a Connection with Source and are Self-Sustaining beings. (200 is the vibration of Courage and 250 is Neutrality, so this is where we have the Courage to follow our paths and true selves, but we are also Non-Attached and do not take things personally.)

Taking energy includes the following behaviors: control dramas, guilt, blame, projection, expectations, or addictions to food/sleep/sex. Humans take energy from one another all day long through these lower-frequency behaviors. Anytime we are embodying a lower frequency, we are in an energy taking state. Even being caught in a lower thought loop is a form of taking energy. You may be able to feel someone close to you who is in lower frequency thoughts, as that lower energy begins to emit from them, perhaps even causing you to get a headache or feel agitated.

Transforming this Programming takes time and comes from Self-Awareness and Transparency. Being totally honest with yourself about what your frequency currently is will help you accept where you are. This neutralizes the energy From Denial to Acceptance.

Here's an example: if I am angry (150 level vibration), I am in a life-draining state. If I am in denial that I am angry by saying, "no I'm fine", or I stuff down the anger and pretend everything is okay, I will sink even lower in vibration. However, if I acknowledge to myself that I am angry, and I accept that this is my current state, I neutralize the energy. I become an observer of myself, rather than being caught up in my emotional state. This immediately begins to transform the energy, and I rise in frequency.

If this is one of your Core Programmings, you will have a hard time sitting still with no distractions. That is a clear sign that you are in a state of needing to take energy. Practice your Conscious Breathing (in through the nose and out through the mouth), Cut Cords with all thought, and Find a Place of Stillness Within. Once you begin to Master your Frequency and can Stay Centered and Present, without the need to distract yourself or move or fidget, you can then move through your day in centeredness.

Mastering your Vibration to stay in a Life-Enhancing State is a Daily Practice. Once you realize everything outside of you is also within you, you Become a Master of Your Own Energy.

INCUBUS & SUCCUBUS ENERGY

Incubus/Succubus is a particular form of taking energy through words, touch, and sex. It's a common energy that comes through in flirting. It is seduction through both obvious and subtle forms. This energy wants attention, validation, and to physically take energy from another.

This can come through in either a masculine or feminine being who uses very enticing words, often having a particular frequency in their voice that can be described as sexy or lustful. This can also come through touching, even casually. It is a mechanism of flirting that seeks to casually touch another – on the arm, or back, or hand – literally taking energy through touch.

Sex is the most obvious example of how this energy comes through. Unless BOTH parties are holding a frequency of Unconditional Love (500 level vibration), there will be some sort of taking energy through a sexual exchange. Because the act of sex is so intimate in nature, energy cords are literally created between the two beings, and physical, emotional, and spiritual energy is exchanged. If one being is holding trauma, wounding, low frequencies, toxins, etc., this will transfer to the other being. There is always one party who is holding a higher vibration than the other, and this vessel gets siphoned from. Most often this is the feminine getting siphoned from due to feminine vessels holding more yin energy, which carries more energies of Love, Compassion, and Heart Opening. However, this can also easily come through a feminine who is in the lower energies of sexual manipulation or jealousy.

To transform this energy, one must truly look at their intentions and energy when speaking, touching, or engaging in sex with another being. If there is lust energy, control, jealousy, vanity, validation, or any other low frequency intent, it is an immediate taking of energy.

We, as a Collective, must now Lead with Our Hearts instead of our bodies. Although we are still on a physical journey, the sexual energy of Humanity will be transformed into an energy of Pure Love. Because Sexual Energy is the Energy of Creation, this is how the Cabal siphoned so much from the Collective, through sexual/lust energy.

For many on the Spiritual Path, they will go through a phase of celibacy. This is a personal choice, yet essential for anyone on the path of truly transforming their Programming. There must be a solitary period where one has no external influences of energy. This allows you moments to Feel Fully into the Energy Within You, and to Cut Cords with all other beings who could be affecting your energy system. This allows you to Take Your Power Back and Harness Your Source Energy through Creative Expression, rather than unconsciously taking energy.

CHILDHOOD TRAUMA

Childhood trauma can be from physical, emotional or mental abuse. However, trauma also presents itself through additional ways, as it comes from wounding, and all human beings are wounded, in one way or another, due to the Programming of their parents and their DNA line. The wounds of repression, guilt, shame, rejection, denial, abandonment, and betrayal, for example, play out in every single family.

Once we realize that all trauma is just karmic residue presenting through our DNA, we stop taking it personally.

The first step in healing trauma is to Forgive. Forgive those who have caused you trauma or wounding because they themselves are traumatized and wounded. Next, Take Accountability for all your experiences. This does NOT mean you are at fault, or you are to blame for the trauma you've experienced, but you must Accept and Embrace that Your Higher-Self Agreed to Such Experiences in order to then transform you.

Before we incarnate on Earth, we are well aware of the karma we are taking on as part of our contract for awakening. Our Higher Selves sign contracts based on the highest service to the whole, not what is best for us on an individual level (such as wants, needs and desires). To transform the trauma that we have taken on, our life journey is largely focused on our physical vessels and what triggers them.

Trauma gets stored in the body as physical density, illness, disease, and pain. This also creates emotional triggers, fears, anxiety, and other lower emotional responses (basically any emotion at the 200 level or lower on the Vibrational Scale).

This is a lot to unpack, so having Patience with Ourselves is essential. Noticing Where the Trauma is Stored in Our Body and what emotional triggers it creates can help us learn to Embrace the Triggers, which show us exactly what needs to be Healed. Then we can breathe deeply into those parts of ourselves, bring them forward, face them, and Love them again.

If this is your Core Programming, most of your Healing work will be aimed at Overcoming Your Triggers and Healing Your Nervous System.

CHILDISH BEHAVIOR

Childlike and childish are two very different frequencies. Childlike Wonder is an energy of excitement and a joy for life, filled with open curiosity and acceptance. It is organic, open, loving, and innocent. Childish behavior, on the other hand, comes from the wounded child within us being denied its wants, needs or desires. It is our reactionary behavior to not feeling supported, safe, nurtured or Loved. We learn these childish behaviors through our parents.

Transforming childish behavior involves Taking Accountability for the Energy and then Looking at Your Reactionary Patterns. *Do you often throw tantrums, get agitated, or act passive aggressively, when you do not get what you want? Are you resistant to taking accountability, apologizing, or letting things go?*

To transform this, one must focus on Responding Rather Than Reacting. Responding involves acknowledging when we have an emotional trigger, breathing, and pausing before we then respond. We do not react out of impulse or anger. We choose the higher road in all situations, no matter how much the other person or experience is triggering us.

If this is your Core Programming, your communication style will go through a transformation. You have not learned how to Effectively Communicate What You Are Feeling and What You Are Asking For. Instead of communicating vulnerably, you resort to reactionary behavior or outbursts, which is a way of taking energy and/or getting a response from another person to get your way in a situation. Work on Communicating How You Are FEELING, rather than what triggered you, and you will be able to transform this Programming.

ROBOTIC HABITS & BEHAVIOR

Due to the way society has Programmed us to live our lives, this is a big issue for most of the Collective. We live very robotic lives that are filled with linear time schedules, routines, and auto-pilot behaviors. This keeps us from being in the Present Moment of Now, which is organic, intuitive and in the perfect flow of nature.

Most of our routines and behaviors are actually outside of the flow of nature by design. We have to un-program ourselves to even function in this inorganic, rigid way of being. To transform this, we must first reflect on our current lives. *How much of our day is done on autopilot? How many things do we do exactly the same, every day, at the same time?*

There is a difference between discipline and robotic, and that comes with Discernment. Discipline is a Divine Trait that entails Being Consistent with yourself, your Spiritual Disciplines, and your Soul Work. However, when it becomes linear, repetitive, forced, or overly structured, then we are becoming robotic.

If this is one of your Core Programmings, focus on how much of your thought process is linear. *Are you always thinking logically, trying to plan things or figure things out?* Start getting in tune with your body, and you will feel into doing certain things. Allow Your Body and Intuition to Guide You on What is Best To Do in Any Certain Moment Versus Forcing Yourself To Do Something. Of course, also Notice Where You Have Resistance To Doing Something – maybe the EGO not wanting you to expand or go outside your comfort zone versus not feeling guided to actually do that particular thing. Start by mixing up your routine and see how it makes you feel. Anything That Feels Repetitive or Robotic May Need To Be Shaken Up so that you can evolve to the next level.

DISRESPECT or HATRED TOWARDS THE FEMININE or MASCULINE

Our society has long pinned the masculine and feminine against one another, which is also a direct reflection of the inner battle we have going on between our inner masculine and inner feminine. The yin (feminine) and the yang (masculine) are complimentary and harmonious in every way. However, due to the suppression of the feminine energy, the masculine have come to over-power and reject the feminine energy, while the feminine have built up anger and resentment towards the masculine. This creates a severe energetic imbalance within each of us, which then creates all sorts of dysfunctions outside of us, such as gender confusion, sexual confusion, and trauma.

Hatred of the feminine runs very deep in BOTH men and women. We have been taught to not only suppress but to also reject and mock the feminine energy. This is why most feminine beings now embody the dark feminine energy instead of the Divine Mother energy. The feminine were suppressed from expression and dominated as the "weaker" gender simply because Feminine Energy Holds More Empathy, Compassion, and the Abilities to Bring Healing and Receiving. This created hatred in the masculine because the feminine are holding the energy they seek within themselves but cannot access.

The feminine reacted to the pure Divine Feminine energy being rejected by becoming the Dark Feminine, using the power of sex, lust, manipulation, or bitch or victim-based behaviors in order to feel Love or gain approval. Society now glorifies these lower feminine energies, which is extremely dysfunctional. This has also created the deep hatred for the masculine and their abuse, power over actions, and rejection.

The Truth, though, is that the Divine Masculine is extremely wounded as well. Their own inner feminine has been suppressed, and they are devoid of feeling and true intimacy.

Both these energies – the hatred of masculine and feminine – lie within each and every being. They are more pronounced if the being has also suffered from deep Mother/Father wounds, abuse, or toxic relationships.

These Energies Must Be Healed Within By Getting In Tune With Your Inner Feminine and Inner Masculine. Forgiving Everyone in Your Life who has hurt you, abandoned you, rejected you, and abused you allows this Healing to take place. Loving others unconditionally, understanding that they too are wounded, allows further Healing. Boundaries are also important, as you can Love another but not enable them, refusing to allow them to steal energy from you. The more balanced we get within, the more harmonious our relationships are with one another.

Balanced Harmonics is the perfect inner union of masculine and feminine energies and are as follows:

Masculine: 51% Masculine/49% Feminine
Feminine: 51% Feminine/49% Masculine

GAY/TRANSGENDER CONDITIONING

This is by far the most controversial conditioning. While reading this, we suggest you first feel into any reactionary energy that seeks to come through you. Read with an open heart and without judgment. The organic energy of the universe is Yin/Yang (Feminine/Masculine). These are the divine counterparts and complimentary energies that make up everything in the Universe.

As stated above, each masculine in a Balanced Harmonics' State, holds 51% masculine and 49% feminine, and vice versa for the feminine. In a Balanced Harmonics' Union, the masculine and feminine would come together to fit a perfect whole. The issue arises because there are no humans on the planet in Balanced Harmonics. The masculine have been hyper-masculine, with very little inner feminine energy, and the feminine have been hyper-feminine, with very little masculine energy.

Now what we are seeing, however, is the Dark seeking to further disrupt our energetic balance by pushing the masculine to be over feminine, while pushing the feminine to be over masculine. This creates such an energetic confusion and imbalance within, that this inner chaos is expressed through our sexuality and gender identity.

If we look at the design of the human vessel, we will see that it was Divinely Created for the feminine to be the carriers and creators of life, as the feminine is the Creator of the Universe. The masculine was to be the supportive, action-oriented energy, as it is in the Universe. The experience of sexual or gender confusion will always stem from an imbalance within.

THERE IS NO JUDGMENT TO THIS. All Humanity is imbalanced within. It's just expressed in different ways.

There are mainly two reasons why sexual confusion occurs: one is trauma and the other is severe energetic imbalance. These can be inherited through the DNA or can be learned through experiences or the environment. This is why many believe that being gay/bi/etc. is genetic. In a way it is, but it still stems from trauma or imbalance.

When one has a trauma experience with one gender, the body creates an unconscious resistance to that gender, out of fear, or they may unconsciously seek out that gender's approval in order to resolve the internal trauma. For example, if a young boy is sexually abused by an adult man, this could create confusion about his sexuality. He may unconsciously then seek out a masculine being sexually, in order to resolve the confusion he has within, or he may become resistant to the masculine as a whole, struggling to even maintain friendships with them. We Seek to Love What We Cannot Understand … This Is The Design. Similarly, if a young girl is sexually abused by an adult masculine, she may unconsciously hold fear and resentment towards men and will gravitate towards women to find Love, or she may develop a dysfunctional view about sexuality with men, which re-creates the trauma.

The other scenario leading to sexual confusion is a deep energetic imbalance. This is also often inherited or picked up from the environment. For example: if one is born with an energetic imbalance through trauma, substances, or programming of the mother, this will affect the child's development. If you are a feminine, but you feel very masculine internally, you will either then sexually seek out the feminine, in order to balance you out, or you will believe that you are actually a masculine and seek to then change your external vessel.

All of this is simply energetic.

ALL MASCULINE SOULS INHABIT MASCULINE VESSELS & ALL FEMININE SOULS INHABIT FEMININE VESSELS. There is much disinformation regarding the soul and the body. But the Truth is that all souls are either feminine or masculine, and they inhabit vessels that match that essence. We do not switch between masculine and feminine vessels, as this would cause confusion to the soul. (That said, we greatly understand how much interference has occurred in Humanity to cause shame, confusion, and disharmony within one's vessel. We encourage all souls to honor what they feel within and wholeheartedly trust their journey.)

Many believe that the Etheric Realm and Angels are all androgynous and, that as a result, gender is an Earth construct. This is only partly true. The Angelic Realm is BALANCED, so masculine and feminine actually operate more alike than different, as masculine would be 51% masculine and 49% feminine, and feminine would be 51% feminine and 49% masculine. However, they serve very different roles, and these roles cannot be ignored or denied.

In 5D, there are many partners, pairs, and unions that may be of the same gender, as these are soul families and soul pods that choose to exist and co-create together. However, these unions are not sexual.

This is the only EGO-Programming in which we will not write about dissolving or transforming. The reason being is because your feelings and your journey are very specific to your soul contract. Many of you contracted for the experience of being gay, bi, transgender, fluid, etc., and those soul contracts are honored. Again, there is no judgment in this, but rather a deeper awareness.

The biggest dysfunction within this Programming is that it is completely derived on sexual preference. In 5D, there is no sex, there is only Making Love, and even that will be a completely different experience and expression than how we see it here on Earth today.

So, instead of looking at this conditioning as needing to be dissolved or transformed, we instead encourage you to simply become aware of where you are out of balance internally between your inner masculine and feminine, and where there is trauma that is unresolved. Next, We Encourage You to View Your Relationships as Partnerships and Divine Unions that are Not Based on Sex, But on Love, Companionship, Growth and Communication. This will transform any underlying dysfunction and give you a much deeper awareness of the beauty of these connections.

For those who do not feel resonance with the gender of their current vessel, we encourage you to Love Yourself MORE. All parts of you that you do not like, or that perhaps you wish to change, must still be Radically Loved By You. Work To Nourish Yourself, Practice Self-Love Disciplines, Accept Yourself, Forgive Yourself, and Have Compassion for Yourself.

All Unions Between Genders, Identities, Etc. are Divine and Serve as Opportunities for Growth, Healing, and Co-Creation. We Deeply Honor and Respect All Soul Contracts Moving into 5D.

As you continue your journey of Self-Love, may you come to remember that YOU are the most unique, brilliant, and amazing being and that your journey is beautiful, no matter what it looks like.

PREFERENCE TO PAIN & SUFFERING

Here on Earth, we exist in a pain and suffering paradigm, also known as the Karmic Plane. In the 3D world of Earth, we feel separate from God, from others, and from Love. This creates the illusion that we are all separate beings in a separate experience, but this is not our reality. In Truth, we are all part of the SAME Source, living parallel experiences through different lenses. We are learning lessons through our pain and suffering in order to understand the karmic consequences of our thoughts, emotions and actions. Free will is an illusion, as all acts outside of Universal Law must eventually be reconciled and aligned.

The challenge is that because we have been stuck in a linear time and space plane, the karmic lessons we are learning are often lifetimes after the originating karmic action occurred. This creates confusion for the soul. We are unclear why a "bad" thing is happening to us. In Truth, karma is not bad or scary. It's very simply unlearned lessons which will continue to present themselves. We will thus manifest the same experiences lifetime after lifetime until we arrive at realizing the greater lesson. We must ask ourselves, *what within us must be healed, let go of and transformed so we do not have to repeat a particular lesson?*

Because pain and suffering are deeply ingrained into our DNA, we are addicted to them. We often unconsciously reject joyful and loving experiences because they are so different from the pain and suffering we're used to experiencing. We believe things are "too good to be true." This goes into a very deep wound tied to the Programming of Unworthiness, which tells us that we deserve our pain and suffering. This may not be a conscious choice, but we must reflect on the experiences in our lives that we have continued to choose or manifest, which are clues that we are reflecting an addiction to pain and suffering.

To transform this Programming, you must Get to the Root of Your Own Unworthiness. *Reflect upon the experiences you have chosen over and over. How are they reflecting your energy and unhealed parts of yourself?* Then, Choose to Love Yourself, Choose to Break the Pattern of Suffering and Finally Learn the Lessons You Were Meant to Learn.

Embrace greater and grander experiences and know that you are deserving of them.

SUPERIORITY

The partner of Superiority is Judgment. When we have judgments of good/bad, right/wrong, etc., they create a lens in which we see ourselves as better than someone or something else. However, judgement ALWAYS works in both directions. So, if you are judgmental of others or external experiences, you are also judgmental of yourself. It is always a two-way street – how we view the external is always a mirror of how we view our internal.

Superiority, therefore, is simply a mask to cover up our own self-judgment. When we are judgmental of ourselves, we begin to compare ourselves to others or outside ideas in order to rationalize within ourselves why we are BETTER than that other person or thing. It makes us feel better about ourselves. However, when one truly Loves themself, and is embodying Divinity, they see nothing as right/wrong, black/white. Rather, they only see the higher perspective in all things. They would never place themselves above another because that other is them.

To dissolve Superiority, you must Dig Deep into All the Ways in which You Judge Things. These can be quite obvious, but also subtle. If this is a Core Programming, then you likely have both the obvious and the more subtle judgments. Obvious judgments are when you react or are triggered by certain things and immediately feel like “that isn’t right” or “that’s bad”. The more subtle frequencies will present themselves as areas in your life or things about yourself in which you are embarrassed. Anytime you feel embarrassed or humiliated by something about yourself or your experiences, you have created a judgment.

Looking at Everything from a Neutral and Higher Perspective Dissolves Superiority and Judgement. You understand that Earth is a game of trial and error, learning and re-learning. Every soul has set up certain experiences for themselves in order to learn lessons. The Etheric Realm has no concept of what is "moral" or "right/wrong"; there is no such thing. These are concepts of the mind. Once we Respect Every Single Soul's Journey and the Experiences They Choose to Have for themselves, we dissolve the need to judge them or feel the need to place ourselves above them.

THINKING YOU KNOW BETTER

This Programming can go along with Superiority, but it is also deeply ingrained via belief systems. This Programming can often come through those who have a lot of 3D education, but not always. It is the belief that you know more than others. It is a sense of arrogance based on "knowledge" or thinking you know something no one else does. This is such a Deep Programming because everyone wants to prove they know more than everyone else!

The funniest part is that we all share a Collective Consciousness, so we all "know" and are able to access the same amount of wisdom. 3D "knowledge", however, is not real, and most of what we learn in 3D is not even true, therefore, we are extremely arrogant to think we know better.

Those living in and from the mind can only perceive 5-6% of ALL ENERGY, compared to those who have expanded their Consciousness, who can see anywhere between 15-40%. Even then, we have not reached the capacity to being able to see 50% of all energy. Therefore, we know nothing!

To best transform this Core Programming, utilize the mantra *"I don't know shit."* Use it over and over, every time you feel yourself going into the energy of "I know better." Understand that we all have internal knowing, experience, and wisdom to share, but this must come from a place of non-attachment, not arrogance. Allow others their journey, allow others to develop their own Intuition of what resonates with them and what does not, and release your need to control.

Practice Listening More Than You Speak. Do Not Make Assumptions, and instead, listen and seek to arrive at a deeper and greater understanding of life. Share Your Wisdoms from the Place of Non-Attachment and Release Your Need to Convince Others You are Right or Seek Validation for Being Right.

ENTITLEMENT

Entitlement comes from having a lack of boundaries. We often think of Entitlement as for beings who are "spoiled" or "demanding", however, we all hold different levels of Entitlement. Entitlement is believing that we deserve a particular thing, person, experience, or action, and we take it personally when we are denied that thing.

For example: many parents believe they are ENTITLED to dictate their child's life, and that the child must make choices and actions to make them happy or because they (as the parents) demand it. Another example: many beings believe they are entitled to energy from others, and this can be expressed through guilt, validation, or dumping energy. They believe they are entitled to your energy and that, if you do not please them, listen to them, dump your energy into them, enable them, or coddle them, you have somehow "hurt them."

Entitlement comes from expectations of others as well as ingrained belief systems about the way the world functions. If we do a certain thing, or follow the rules, or make the "right" choices, then we are taught that we are entitled to a certain result. This deeply frustrates us and creates a brat-like energy when we do not get the results we were expecting. I often refer back to the phrase, *"I am entitled to my opinion."* That phrase holds so many belief systems within it. Essentially, we are saying that we deserve to have a belief system about something, and not to be questioned on that belief system. We think we are entitled to our illusion, and no one must break that illusion for us. How ironic!

To break this Programming, we must Start Shifting the Perspective from Expectation to Acceptance. The only person we can ever change is ourself. We must have stronger Boundaries, stronger Self-Love Practices, and stronger Acceptance. When we let go of expectations, assumptions, or EGO desires, and Love ourselves, we feel WORTHY, not entitled. We know we are Worthy of Love, Joy, and Happiness, but not entitled to anything. We earn our grandness through being grand ourselves.

If this is one of your Core Programs, you must look at your needs, wants, desires, and expectations, reflected upon them and dissolving them. Once you stop feeding the EGO's needs, wants and desires, you realize you stop seeking so many external things. This is where you stop embodying entitlement. You are no longer seeking anything nor expecting anything. Instead, you Stay in the Frequency of Acceptance, Allowance, and Gratitude.

SELF-IMPORTANCE

All human beings are in self-importance, to some extent. Those who have Awakened and are Consciously on the Path of Service have dissolved most of their Self-Importance, but it still comes up from time to time. We are in Self-Importance because we are in the mindset of separateness. When we feel separate, we view the world through our own bubble. We think about US, not about the whole, which causes us to be solely focused on serving our EGO needs, wants and desires.

If we look, everyone in society is focused on themselves or their families, alone. We put ourselves and our nuclear family over all others and all things. This is a deep sense of ancient tribalism preventing us from remembering that We Are All One, Large, Interconnected Soul Family. Once we remember that we are all One, the way we live our lives will completely change.

To dissolve self-importance is simple: be in service.

Being In Service to The Greater Good Dissolves Your Frequency of Self-Importance. Being in service is also doing your own Inner Work,

Being Kind and Compassionate to yourself and others, Transforming Yourself. If you are dedicating your energy to transforming yourself, to being your grandest version, and to helping and assisting others in your unique way, then you are completely in alignment with your Higher Self.

If Self-Importance is one of your Core Programmings, you will have to actively monitor your wants, needs and desires. Take stock of all the things in your life that truly are not important. Start spending less time on these things and more on what is truly good for your soul. The More You Continue to Make Higher Choices, the More You Will Naturally Move into a Service-Based Life.

DELUSIONS OF GRANDEUR

This Programming runs alongside Arrogance and the Spiritual & Super Ego. It presents itself as the belief that you are above others, more important than others, and are more "special." This often shows up in the spiritual community, scientific community, or any community in which people develop an identity about who they are and what their role is. Any attachment you may have to who you are, or what your role is, must be let go of.

To transform this Programming requires both Compassion and a Deeper Understanding of Oneness. There is a balance between knowing you are Worthy of Love, and knowing that you are important, versus falling into the trap of feeling MORE important than any other being. We all have different roles and paths, as some may have the role of the leader or teacher, while others have the role of being the mirror, the student, or the supporter. We are all equal in our roles yet have various responsibilities.

Take Accountability and Responsibility for Your Role, Knowing in Your Heart Your Purpose, But Also Let Go Of Any Notion or Thought That Your Role is More Important Than Any Other.

We can see how this programming created the external manifestations of Royalty, Monarchs, Elites, and Celebrities. We all are seeking to feel that specialness about ourselves and because we cannot find it, we create external versions to strive for.

If this is a Core Programming for you, Focus On Having Compassion for Others, While Also Seeing The Beauty of Each Being's Journey, Role and Essence. See the Higher Self Within Every Single Being, See the Beauty Of Everything Ever Created, and There You Will Find the True Nature Of Oneness and Harmony.

FANTASY

Fantasy is focusing on anything that is outside of the present moment. If we are thinking about the past, contemplating or worrying about the future, constantly in thought about things that are not important to our present moment or becoming attached to external information, then we are living in Fantasy.

Dreams, Visions, and Goals can, of course, be Imagined, especially during Meditation, and we can then Connect with the Dream we wish to Manifest, Matching Our Frequency to that Dream. This is different than Fantasy, where we are chasing or seeking something that never manifests into physicality. The Illusions of the past and future keep us in a fog.

If your thoughts, and being outside the present moment, is a struggle for you, then your focus needs to be on Cutting Cords with these thoughts and then beginning to Master Being Quiet. Stillness and Presence dissolves everything that is not real. It brings us back to Center, where anything that is real will always be. Anything real will always return, so we do not have to keep thinking about it.

If this is one of your Core Programmings, Practice Writing Everything Down. Write down your feelings, your thoughts, your experiences, your questions, your synchronicities … EVERYTHING. Once You Write It Down, Let It Go. Do not keep revisiting it. Whatever is not real will dissolve away, and whatever is real will always come back. You can always ask your Angels for Confirms and

Synchronicities as well as to give you guidance and confirmation of anything you are feeling or questioning.

NEEDING TO BE RIGHT

The judgments of right versus wrong are non-existent in higher realms. Everything just is, and there is always a higher purpose for it. When we feel the need to be right, or we fear being wrong, what we are saying is that "wrong=bad", and this is then taken personally as a reflection of self.

The mind makes us personalize everything, even though everything is just a reflection of everything else. So, there is no "personal". If we are wrong, we believe this is a negative reflection of ourselves as a being, which is an illusion created by the mind.

The EGO always has to be right because it can only function in linear, concrete ways. Things are either left or right, black or white, square or circle. It works as a computer, defining things based on the category it places them in. Everything has to have proof, an answer, and an ending, contrary to everything Creation is. Creation is always changing, always evolving. Everything is multi-dimensional, unknown, always dying and being born again.

To dissolve this Programming, Notice Where You are On The Defensive, needing to have the last word and always wanting to debate. These are signs that you are attached to being right. Begin seeing your thoughts, beliefs, and opinions as just a passing energy. They are not you, nor are they part of you. They're simply wavelengths that have come to you to be interpreted by you. This allows you to Let Go of Needing an Answer and instead, embracing that you do not and will never know anything. This is the beauty of the unknown, and it requires a Deep Surrender and Trust.

If this is one of your Core Programs, utilize the mantra *"I don't know shit"* as often as you need to. Be open to all new information and Truths, and Only Hold Onto What Resonates, Letting The Rest Go. Allow your childlike wonder to keep you in Curiosity and Openness.

CONTROLLING

Control is an energetic that we embody when we are in fear of something. Usually, we have underlying wounding and trauma that we wish to avoid being triggered, so we control others and our environment. Giving up control is one of the most challenging Programs to dissolve. Once you begin noticing all the ways in which you exhibit control, it takes a lot of Surrender and Patience with yourself to let go of it.

The most obvious way this presents itself is in relationships. One or both beings are usually exerting some level of control over their partner and their choices/actions. This can also present itself through parent/child dynamics, where very often, either the parent or child is controlling the other through manipulation, emotional guilt, or expectations. Other ways this presents are through OCD, micro-managing, or anxiety, often displayed in career settings with bosses as well as in your everyday life.

To dissolve control, we must start surrendering. We must see our need for control and perfection as simply reflecting our deep fears of not being good enough, or having our wounds triggered, or being uncomfortable.

By controlling, we also do not allow miracles to occur. Miracles and surprises can only come when we are in surrender, willing to embrace the unknown.

If this is one of your Core Programmings, begin by getting in tune with your body. Feel Where There is Tension and Pain, often in the upper back, shoulders, and neck. Breathe into those spaces and release the tension energy. When our body is in fight or flight (survival mode), we go into control even deeper. When you feel control coming up, Breathe, Surrender, and Repeat the Mantra *"I accept, embrace, and allow."*

UNGRATEFUL

Humanity is widely Ungrateful. The energy of Gratitude naturally brings more blessings to you. The reason we have poverty, lack, and exist in survival mode is a reflection of our fractured Consciousness which is in lack, fear, and ungratefulness. We don't appreciate the beauty of life, instead we seek things that are not heart-filled, such as material possessions, money, clothes, sex, and entertainment.

We are Ungrateful for our host, Mother Earth, who provides endlessly for us. All we do is take her resources and pillage her into barrenness. This is the epitome of being Ungrateful.

Our Higher Selves create a Divine Plan for our lives – certain experiences and connections we agree to have for our greatest soul growth – yet, we are Ungrateful for the challenges. Instead, we complain, play the victim, and find a way to place blame.

To dissolve ungratefulness, we must Start Seeing Everything in the Higher Perspective, Start Appreciating Life Itself – the Source Spark that lives within everything and comes back to our hearts. When we Start Enjoying the Simple Things such as the sun, cool water, a hot shower, a cup of tea, the birds chirping in the morning, the feeling and sounds of the ocean, then we will truly be Grateful for all we have.

If this is one of your Core Programmings, Start a Gratitude Journal. Commit yourself to writing in your journal each day the things that you are Grateful for. Repeat the mantra, *"I am grateful,"* and bring that energy into your heart center. The more you focus on Gratitude, the more you truly feel it, and that is where the magic begins to happen. Start saying *thank you* for the lessons, the challenges, and the people who hurt you. Say *Thank You* To It All.

NO ACCOUNTABILITY

No Accountability stems from Denial and the Need to be Right. Taking Accountability does not make you "wrong", it makes you Divine. Most beings are afraid to take Accountability because they do not want to feel blamed, guilty, or wrong. Once we see these thoughts as illusionary, we realize that Taking Accountability is the Divine Action as everything is a reflection of ourselves. So, by Taking Accountability, we help transform that energy for all.

For example: if you see someone who is acting in a way that is not in alignment with Love, our first reaction is normally to point it out to the person, complain about the behavior, or blame them for the way it has affected us. Instead, try first Taking Accountability within YOURSELF for where their actions are a reflection of you and how you have embodied that same energy. Once you've done that, then you can work to transform that energy, and in doing so, you can share with the other person your observations, how you are Taking Accountability, and how you're working to resolve any issues created. This is true leadership by example.

If this is one of your Core Programs, you will need to feel deeply into what the root of your lack of accountability is. *Are you afraid to be wrong? Were you blamed as a child for things that weren't your fault? Are you afraid of being judged or rejected?* Once you can identify the root of your resistance, then you can actively change it.

If anyone calls something out in you, brings something to your awareness, or triggers something in you, follow the process of first Taking Accountability, reflecting, and then committing to changing yourself and your responses. You do not need to prove anything to the other person, nor do you need to apologize or feel guilty. You Simply Own Your Truth and Your Energy, as that is all you can truly be accountable for.

SPREADING OR PARTICIPATION IN GOSSIP

Gossip is speaking about the lower aspects of someone else, without being able to compassionately call them out. Gossip energy, at its root, is just a way beings cover up their own dysfunctions and issues by focusing on someone else's. Venting can sometimes be confused as Gossiping. Venting is the process of sharing an experience, or sharing about an interaction with another being, expressing your feelings and emotions in order to process them. There is no judgment in the process of venting, as you're simply expressing your feelings.

To transform Gossip, one should always first reflect on one's intention for sharing something. *Is this being sharing to give an awareness, or share a perspective? Or is this information being shared in order to judge or shame someone else or a situation?* If the Gossip involves your opinion about another being, the question is, *have you called this person out with compassion on their dysfunction?* If the answer is no, then you should consider doing that first.

Feel into the root of the gossip. *Do you feel some level of inferiority or unworthiness? Does focusing on someone else's dysfunction make you feel better?* Be aware of the energy with which you share things or speak about others. Be conscious of your intent and Realize That Every Being is Doing the Best They Can in the Consciousness They are In.

JEALOUSY

Jealousy is extremely common, especially amongst the feminine. The root of Jealousy is desire and attachment. When we are jealous in a relationship, we have the fear of "losing" our partner to someone else because we are attached to them. It's also rooted in a deep competition, which the Dark have plagued the feminine with to always keep them against one another. When we are Non-Attached, however, which means we Love Unconditionally, we do not feel jealousy, but rather Allowance.

When we are Jealous of another person or situation, it is because we desire to be like that person or to have what the person has. The energy of desire comes from the mind's place of comparison. We are constantly comparing ourselves to others and desiring something we think is better than what we have or who we are.

To dissolve Jealousy, one must truly feel into the nature of that physical experience. Every single being's soul is a fractal of Source, which means, every being is Divine and perfect at their core. The vessels we chose to come down in, and the experiences we chose to have, have now shaped our physical expression of our essence. We judge and compare ourselves based on our vessel, our 3D lives, and external circumstances, when In Truth, We Are All ONE At Our Cores.

If this is one of your Programmings, you must focus on your own Self-Worth. The more you Love yourself, the more you dissolve jealousy. When you recognize the unique brilliance within you, you begin to see that same unique brilliance in all others. We realize that our exact essence can never be recreated, and our exact path can never be taken from us. It is our destiny. And thus, we Stop Competing, and we Start Appreciating.

VANITY

Vanity at its core is a deep lack of Self-Love and Unworthiness. It is our human mind's arrogance to think that we are all separate and are having separate experiences. This is how Vanity takes hold – we believe that we are our bodies, clothes, car, house, partner, etc. We don't Love our souls enough, and we don't feel Worthy, so we cover that up through our over-focus on all-things external to us, such as our beauty and possessions.

You may find yourself constantly obsessing about your skin, hair, body shape, clothes, makeup, tattoos, etc. This over-focus on the external creates an obsession with it, which keeps us further and further away from really seeing our own soul. This can also translate to an over-focus on our image or persona. In this day and age, most teens to early 20-somethings are stuck in Vanity. All they care about is how something looks on the surface.

To dissolve Vanity, you need to Focus on the Internal Rather Than the External. Anytime your focus gets pulled towards an external thing, immediately bring it back into yourself. Focus on how you FEEL. Bringing Spiritual Disciplines into your life will also assist this process. This brings the energy inward, focusing on nourishing your soul rather than your external. Tools like the Mirror Technique (I AM Affirmations), Journaling, and Meditation are great tools to keep the focus on your inner self.

If this is one of your Core Programmings, you will likely need to cut off many of your external habits. For instance, if you are overly focused on your appearance, you will need to change your routines. If you are spending too much time each day doing things with the intention to make you look a certain way (i.e., makeup, hair, working out, tanning, getting dressed), then you will have to cut out those routines. Spend as Much Time as Possible Being Organic and In Your Natural State. Start to appreciate everything you have to offer inside of you and start detaching from the outside.

LACK OF BEAUTY

This goes hand-in-hand with Vanity. Lack of Beauty works two ways: seeing a lack of internal beauty within yourself and not seeing the beauty of things outside yourself. When this presents as an internal issue, one cannot see the beauty within themselves. They are in Vanity, so they only focus on the outside, or they find themself beautiful on the outside but cannot see the beauty of their soul. This can also present itself externally in one who never sees the positive in life and is thus rather pessimistic.

To dissolve this Programming, one should follow the techniques for escaping Vanity, as well as start to Appreciate the Beauty of The Little Things. Appreciate the little things about yourself – your laugh, your eyes, the way you smile, your heart, your kindness, or your humor. Then start to notice the little things in the external world – seeing a butterfly, a sunset, your dog, or a beautiful flower.

One of Your Greatest Tools Here Will Be ART. Art is the expression of an emotion, a feeling, a vision, or an experience. It is the bridge that brings life to a story. When you allow yourself to freely create art, such as drawing, coloring, painting, weaving, knitting, pottery, carving, etc., you start to see what beauty truly is. It is a pure expression of Love.

DESIRE

Needs, Wants and Desires are the basis of the EGO. However, these Desires can actually never be fulfilled because they come from a place of lack, the void that can never be filled. When we Desire something, it's like a craving. We are seeking something we feel is going to make us feel better, or temporarily Heal our pain, or fill the void we feel inside. This presents itself in different ways, such as Desiring a person, a food, a certain role, or a fantasy.

This can also present as Wanting to be Desired. We can seek to be Desired by another being, Desired in a way that others "need" us or we are sought after for some skill or power we possess. The Want of Being Desired stems from the need for validation and a lack of Self-Love.

To dissolve Desire, we first have to be able to recognize it. Whenever we feel that deep craving for something, and we want it NOW, that is a sure sign that it is Desire and not an aligned want. Stop, take a breath, and feel into what it is you are ACTUALLY Desiring. *If you are desiring sex, are you really seeking Love, connection, or intimacy?* Those are very different things. If you are Desiring certain foods or sweets, is there an emotion you're seeking to numb or are you seeking to escape feeling something? If you are Desiring a certain job or role in life, are you really seeking validation of your worth?

If this is one of your Core Programs, you must get honest with yourself about the things you are Desiring. The biggest challenge is to actively not feed the blackhole of desire and instead, to take a step back, wait, and move through the emotions of what you're feeling, rather than continuing to seek for instant gratification. The more you uncover what it is you are truly seeking, you will Stop Desiring Things and Instead

Move Into Allowing Things Naturally Aligned For You To Come To You.

VALIDATION

Validation is the need for others to agree with you, to give you confirmations, and to give you confidence. This is all based on a lack of trust in God and oneself. When we do not trust Source or ourselves, we question everything. We want to make sure we are pretty, successful, a good person, or are doing the right thing. We have a whole laundry list of things we want to be Validated for. Why? Because we do not trust our own Intuition, our actions, and our feelings.

Validation also covers up a deep insecurity of unworthiness. When we feel unworthy, we constantly seek an external Validation of our worthiness. This happens often with children who grow up with overbearing parents. They want to gain their parents' Validation, gifts, or approval.

Many feminine fall into needing Validation from the masculine, because they have not come to fully Love their own feminine essence. Masculine will seek Validation often from each other or through external things such as money, status, title, etc.

To dissolve Validation, we have to start trusting ourselves. The first step in Learning to Trust Yourself is By Trusting Source, fully knowing that all things are perfect and Divinely Designed. When we trust that ultimately, Everything Serves the Highest Good, we loosen the control of thinking we need to fix, overcome, or seek something. When we Start Trusting Source, our connection to it opens up more, and we begin developing a connection with our hearts, our Angels, and our Higher Selves.

Being able to feel this means quieting our internal chatter enough that our Intuition can share with us. When we have a feeling or a nudge to do something or take a certain action, or to not take an action, we must Trust That Nudge. THERE IS NO RIGHT OR WRONG CHOICE, EVER. EITHER WAY WE CHOOSE, IT WILL BE A

LESSON OR A BLESSING THAT IS PERFECT FOR US IN THAT MOMENT. When we doubt ourselves and seek validation, we will never have a true sense of self and will constantly be giving away our power.

If this is one of your Core Programs, reflect on all the ways in which you seek validation. Start affirming things for yourself by committing to your own Truth and trusting your feelings, without question. Notice where you feel the need to constantly people-please, apologize, or explain yourself. Ask yourself if you need to Set More (Or Better) Boundaries. Focus on the Mirror Technique and I AM Affirmations. Begin speaking to your heart in a loving and positive way.

WANTING TO FOLLOW OR BE FOLLOWED

This Programming shows itself deeply in religious and spiritual communities. The religions of the world have created a false god that is outside of ourselves, and that must be worshipped. This is the complete opposite of the true nature of Source, which is a feminine essence, and is the yin/internal energy. WE ARE ALL GOD WITH GOD. The spiritual community also created this energy of wanting to be followed by placing themselves in a higher or more prestigious position than the rest of Humanity. Because they woke up first, they believe they should be followed, that they know something more than everyone else.

True Trust-Based Followings are about Unity.

This Program can present itself in a few ways. If you want to follow others, then you have a deep energy of needing to be saved. You do not trust yourself, nor have you developed your own Empowerment. You would rather follow another, who tells you what to do, than to have to make your own choices and follow your own guidance. Religious Programming would fall under this category.

Wanting to be followed presents itself as someone who seeks to have minions. We sometimes see this in teenagers, where one feminine or masculine rises as the leader of a group of friends, and everyone follows that person. This is an unconscious God Complex, which has been woven into our DNA as the need of having or being a god to be worshipped and followed.

To dissolve both of these energies, as they are two sides of the same coin, one must dissolve all internal savior programming, realizing that You Are One With God, And So, God Is Not Above You Or Even Outside Of You, But Rather, Is Part Of You.

We are all empowered and responsible for ourselves. We are not responsible for any other being on the planet, this even includes our children and family. Each and Every Soul on This Planet is Responsible For Their Own Path and Journey, As Per Their Contract.

If this is one of your Core Programmings, then you must take back your power. Focus on Empowering Yourself and Letting Go Of Any Illusion of Obligation to others or the urge to try and "save" others. This is the same frequency as the lack of empowerment. Be the Best You Can Be and Focus Solely on Yourself and Your Own Growth. You will come to feel the depths of how Divine you are, without needing to follow another or be followed.

FAKE

Being Fake is not being genuine and is also associated with compulsive lying. When a being is Fake, there is a deep discomfort in embracing who they are. There is self-hatred that is creating a fear of being real and authentic. This could be an irrational self-hatred, based on paranoid thoughts, or this could be based in guilt or shame, due to something done or experienced in life.

Those who are Fake cannot be vulnerable or authentic, and they often lie about even small things, telling many white lies. Fear of being judged or rejected can also be at the heart of this energetic frequency.

You will know you have this Programming, if you find yourself saying one thing but really thinking another, lying about small things out of embarrassment or compulsion, or pretending to like a thing or person because you are afraid to express yourself.

To dissolve fakeness requires transparency. *Whole Truth heals.* When we can openly express ourselves, even our biggest fears or thoughts, we dissolve the barrier between "us" and "them". When we are Authentic, we fully own who we are, our story, our challenges and accomplishments. We see the beauty in everything, so we have no reason not to be real.

If this is one of your Core Programmings, there is something you are hiding from others or yourself that you are afraid to face. If this is a belief about yourself, then it must be examined and seen for the illusion that it is. If this is guilt or shame over an experience or action, you must extend Forgiveness to yourself, all others, and all situations. Once you begin to peel back these layers, you will organically Become More Open and Authentic With Others, as you will have no fear of anything.

REVERENCE OF THE MIND

This Programming most often occurs in the education and elite circles of our 3D society. Those who place a higher value on "education", degrees, status, accomplishments, knowledge, and words are those who have Reverence of the Mind. Essentially, these beings favor the mind and the analytics of things, while pushing away feelings and emotions. When one has Reverence of the Mind, they often strive to be the smartest or most knowledgeable person in the room, often being overly concerned with things like credentials, grammar, and big words.

We, as a society, have put our focus on the mind rather than the heart. That said, a being with this Programming actually values the mind over the heart. It is the belief that analyzing, linear thinking, and logic are more important than Feeling, Compassion, Love and

Empathy. These beings have a deep lack of feeling and must go through the process of once again getting in tune with their hearts.

To dissolve this Core Programming, one must focus on their heart and their feelings. For those who are very disconnected from their hearts, the first step is to deeply feel your body. Spend moments each day focusing on your breathing, in through the nose and out through the mouth. Breathing Love in and Breathing Love out. Begin to notice the sensations of your body, which can be pain, stiffness, aching, tightness, or tension. Keep breathing into these places, cutting cords with your thoughts, feeling into the emotions stored in these places in your physical body.

Different emotions get stored in different places; for example, anger typically gets stored in the sacral or solar plexus, fear gets stored in the root chakra and legs, grief gets stored in the chest and arms, and trauma can be stored in the throat and mouth.

If this is one of your main Programmings, you must Cut Cords with Linear Thinking. Commit yourself to focusing solely on how you feel, and not on what you think. This process takes Patience and Practice, returning yourself to feeling and receiving, activating your feminine energy, which restores your true brain/heart connection. Understand that the mind is an illusion and was created only to serve the fight or flight survival mode.

In Truth, There Is No Seeking, No Answers, No Logic. Creation Is Made Out Of Love And The Unknown.

SEEKING REVERENCE

Seeking Reverence often displays itself as one who has a belief system about Divinity. We see this often in churches and some spiritual communities. We have beliefs like wearing white, talking softly, wearing certain jewels, holding silence, whatever we've determined makes us Divine and a being others should revere. This is an illusionary belief system that creates a worship energy.

When we are Seeking Reverence, we are seeking for others to see us on a pedestal. This is different than wanting to be desired, or wanting to be feared, this is more of a God Complex. These beings are seeking to be held up above others and to be seen as a holy or pristine figure. All this is based on fantasy and illusion and what are false belief systems around God and Divinity.

To dissolve this Programming, one must realize that all thoughts of the way one "should be" are based in the mind. Thinking that you are a godly or holy figure that should be revered means you truly don't understand God. Divinity is Raw, Real, Honest, Playful, Expressive, and Organic, and It Follows No Rules or Constructs.

If this is one of your Core Programmings, you must feel into the root of wanting to be revered. *Do you actually believe you are God with God and that you as a soul are perfect and Divine?* The answer is likely no, which is why you are seeking to be revered. It is a much deeper form of validation that stems from the belief that we are separate from God. When we heal that wound, we drop all need of being revered.

REVERANCE OF ANIMALS

Many do not feel they have a Reverence of Animals, but this is a common Programming. It's when you place animals above human beings, or above all other things. We see this commonly in extreme animal activists, where they place the safety and "rescuing" of animals even above human lives. It's a deep form of savior programming and victim consciousness. However, this can also present itself subtly with those who own animals, where they treat the animal as if it were a human being, in some cases, better than they treat themselves or the other humans in the house.

Many do not truly understand animals or their contracts. Animals already exist in Unconditional Love. They are purely in the Present Moment of Now, connected to Source, and exist in 5D frequencies. Animals do not have EGOs, nor a mind; therefore, they function solely in Unity Consciousness, based on their Intuition (what some refer to as instinct). Animals do not experience pain and suffering as we do. Because they exist in Unconditional Love, they do experience pain, but they do not experience suffering. Suffering is when we are attached to pain, which animals cannot be, due to their high frequency.

We as humans suffer, due to our attachments and belief systems. And we project this suffering onto animals, which is why we have the abuse of animals as a reflection of the abuse we put ourselves through. Then, we seek to "save" and "rescue" the animals, due to our inability to see that we must first save ourselves.

Animals have contracted to be on Earth to help Humanity hold a higher frequency and to anchor in Unconditional Love for us. They have also contracted to provide themselves as a food source, and also our companions.

To dissolve this Programming, remember that Animals are Always in Love, we do not need to try and validate them, spoil them, or save them. Now this is NOT to say we should not be striving to care for animals better, and to create safe spaces for them. This is just to say we do not revere animals more than we revere human life. Owners of animals need to look at their dysfunctional tendencies, such as treating them as if they were humans, prioritizing their animals over other humans and other things, obsessing over them rather than focusing on their own well-being.

If this is one of your Core Programmings, you likely need to create more discipline and better boundaries for your animal, or animals in general. Remember, They are Divinely Intelligent, and They Have Their Own Paths and Contracts.

JUSTIFICATION

This Programming pairs with Denial and Needing to be Right. When we are in Denial about something, or we feel the Need to be Right, we are Seeking to Justify ourselves. We refuse to accept accountability and instead, we create illusionary support for why we did or said something. This often presents itself as the need to explain yourself, always having a story for why you did or said something, or an inability to receive a call out from another person.

When we feel the Need to Justify ourselves, it can come from a place of needing to be right, or it can come from the place of the fear of being wrong. These are two sides of the same coin, but they present differently. If you are always over-explaining yourself, wanting another person to see your point of view, fearing what others think, then you have a fear of being wrong. If you refuse to take accountability for things and often get defensive by justifying your actions, then you have a need to be right.

To dissolve this energetic frequency, Start Letting Go Of the Need to be Right and The Fear of Being Wrong. Realize that no one outside of yourself can ever validate you. You must be able to both receive from others and trust yourself. If someone calls you out on something, say, *"thank you ... I take accountability, and I will feel into that."* If you feel into it, and the call out doesn't resonate, then let it go. If it does resonate, then you graciously look at what you can still transform. If you are giving your power away by always justifying and explaining, Pull Your Power Back to Yourself and Honor Others for Their Perspectives, Just Don't Take Them Personally.

If this is one of your Core Programs, Accountability and Empowerment will be your two biggest focuses. The more you Take Accountability, even for things you don't feel responsible for, the easier and more Empowering your life will become. Have Proper Boundaries and Own Your Choices and Truths, and when you feel you have taken on others' opinions or projections, use the mantra *"I return all energy to sender"*.

PROCRASTINATION

This Programming pairs with laziness, as they both delay actions due to resistance or a lack of Self-Love. LOVE-IN-ACTION IS THE HIGHEST VIBRATIONAL FREQUENCY IN EXISTENCE. When we constantly prevent ourselves from taking action, either through resistance, fear, apathy, or laziness, we prevent our own transformation. Our greatest growth will always come from a feeling and an action. When we take action, we are manifesting energy into physicality, which has a profound ripple effect within the Collective.

We often procrastinate due to resistance or fear. We have ideas and dreams we wish to actualize, but we are so unsure of ourselves, or in fear, we stop ourselves from even taking the first step. This is self-sabotage. Our EGO knows once we can take our first step forward, we will make a breakthrough.

We can also procrastinate out of laziness or apathy. When this occurs, our body is trying to tell us something. If we cannot feel the motivation or the passion to move forward in our lives, then this is a signal that there is grief, wounding, or trauma that needs to be released. Nurture Yourself, Honor Your Feelings, and Rest If You Need To. Then Gather Your Strength and Push Yourself to Take a Few Small Steps Each Day in The Direction You Want to Go.

The key to transforming any form of Procrastination is to focus on the immediate small step in front of you, not on the whole staircase. When we focus too much on the bigger picture, we can easily get overwhelmed, which creates fear and resistance. Ask yourself each day, *"what steps can I take today, right now, to move in the right direction?"* Organize your schedule and write down a few things that you can accomplish TODAY. The first step is always the hardest.

If this is one of your Programmings, you will need to establish whether you are self-sabotaging or you are simply internally exhausted. Spend time with yourself, feeling into your dreams, your goals, and what is no longer working in your life. Often times, we need to clear something out so that we can move forward. We can literally feel bogged down by emotional baggage, mental baggage, and physical baggage. Clear out your physical space, take stock of thoughts and emotions that are no longer serving you and then release them. In addition, you can integrate Spiritual Disciplines and Tasks into your daily routine.

BARGAINING

Bargaining occurs when we have a block to truly Giving and Receiving. We may find that we are always seeking to get something for what we give, or to get more out of others. This typically is a cultural or environmental programming that tends to run in specific areas of the world. For instance, in poorer countries that are very reliant on tourism, they are taught to bargain with tourists, focusing on selling as many items as possible.

Bargaining can also occur between friends or business associates. We ask for a favor and, in return, we offer to give something, or we want the other person to give more and us less. There is always bargaining happening in business on some level, and it stems from lack-consciousness and also the desire to "win". If we receive a bargain, such as getting an item on sale, our mind convinces us that we have won something, we came out on top. This is the energy of Bargaining. By the same token, we value things more that are expensive because our mind convinces us that a higher price means a higher value, hence we want to "bargain" to receive something greater for less.

To dissolve this Programming, we must come to the realization that there is no winning. Every Situation Should Be A Win-Win For All Parties, Not A Win-Lose Scenario. Others' Joy is just as important as our own Joy, and others' Fulfillment is just as important as our own. We Should Always Be Seeking For Love To Be Present In All Transactions. Be open to Giving as well as Receiving. Gratefulness also helps dissolve this frequency.

If this is one of your Core Programmings, you may often find yourself in the energy of trying to get what you want, at all costs. Focus On Giving To Others, Without Any Expectations Or Wanting To Receive Back. And When You Receive Something, Receive It With Gratitude And Worthiness, And Do Not Feel You Have To Give Something Back Just For The Sake Of Doing So.

POVERTY CONSCIOUSNESS

Poverty or Lack-Consciousness has been Deeply Programmed into Humanity in order to keep us in survival mode. Whether you are "rich" or "poor" does not matter, all beings hold a certain degree of Poverty Consciousness. This Programming presents itself through fear, anxiety, and the worry of not having enough. The irony is that no matter how much money or possessions we have, we still feel there will never be enough.

The Dark used this Programming to convince us that things like money, resources, food, Love, jobs, etc. are all scarce. This created the competition to survive, as we feel we need to take from others so that we can thrive. In Truth, it is only the belief that something is in lack that actually creates the lack.

A great example of this was during the Pandemic when we were told that certain items, such as toilet paper, were becoming scarce. This created a Poverty Consciousness which caused beings to over-buy and hoard toilet paper, for no reason, thus CREATING the lack. This tactic is often used with other resources as well, like water.

This Programming also presents itself as having the belief that things like Happiness, Stability, Safety, and Support are hard to come by. We believe that we must work hard to earn these things, when really, they are freely given. We become attached to the things that we feel give us these good feelings, refusing to let go because we fear we will never obtain them again.

To dissolve this Programming, we must realize that nothing is ever in lack. The Universe Is Abundant, And We Are Abundant. What we are poor in is Spirituality and Connection to Source. The more we fulfill our connection to God and to our own spirit, the more Abundant we feel and become. The energy of Gratitude also dissolves this lack-consciousness. Once We Start Focusing On All The Blessings We DO Have, The Less We Focus On What We Don't Have.

If this is one of your Core Programmings, understand this is a Genetic Programming that passes down through the DNA. It takes many moments to fully dissolve this, but by focusing on the things that matter to you, such as Family, Love, Service, Joy, and Inspiration, the more fulfilled you will feel, and thus, the more Abundant you'll also feel. Actively flip your belief systems and utilize the mantras of *"I am abundant"*, *"I trust in Source"*, and *"I always have everything I need exactly when I need it."*

ADDICTION TO SUGAR

Many may not think this is a Programming, but it is a very deep one! Although we are all powerful beings, who can transmute anything we eat or drink, sugar was created as a very specific drug to keep us addicted, brain-damaged, and distracted. Sugar is the only food or substance we highly recommend limiting or cutting out altogether. Sugar highly affects our brains and creates an addiction cycle as well as a numbing and escaping mechanism.

Our brains use sugar as a way to fill a void (or need) that is actually emotional. You may notice you crave sugar at particular times of the day or during stressful or emotional moments in your life. If sugar is a daily craving for you, feel into what the sugar means to you. *Are you addicted to the sweet taste? Are you addicted to the energy? Are you trying to create an external joy because it's lacking internally?* There are many reasons we crave sugar, mainly because it triggers the same satisfactions in the brain that drugs and sex do.

To dissolve this addiction, one must first go cold turkey. One cannot balance out an addiction by simply reducing the usage, our system needs to first detox from the addiction, dissolving the physical and emotional attachments to it, and then we can re-integrate it into our lives, with balance.

If this is one of your Core Programs, commit yourself to at least 7 days with no sugar. This will give your body time to purge the toxins out of your system and allow it to stabilize. Feel into the emotional aspect of the addiction and then work to give yourself what you're actually craving, which may be Joy, Energy, Happiness, or the Sweetness of Life.

Once you have dissolved the emotional attachment, and you are coming into balance, each time you are craving sugar, feel into whether or not your body is asking for it energetically, or you are simply giving yourself some Joy. As long as it is ingested with Integrity, sugar can be digested, occasionally.

LINEAR THINKING AND ACTING

The mind can only think in linear terms, meaning it can only relate something to the past or worry/speculate about the future. Linear Thinking includes planning, analyzing, thinking logically, and micro-managing. The Truth, However, Is That Time Is Not Linear. Time Does Not Exist As The Construct We Know It As. Time Is A Spiral, And We Are Always Merging Many Different Timelines And Moments Into The Present. If we are attached to "time" based on the future and the past, we are not in the heart and in the now, so we miss vital opportunities to experience miracles and synchronicities.

When we are in the linear mind, we are not in the flow of the Universe. We miss the signs, the gentle nudges of our Angels, and the miracles that Source is showing us. We plan so much for the future, trying not to re-create the past, but ironically, we are always re-creating the past.

To dissolve this Programming, we have to stay in the Present Moment of Now. This takes Practice and Patience, but it is the key to Opening Our Hearts and entering Full Consciousness. Whenever a thought comes in that is not relevant to the Present Moment of Now, say out loud, *"I cut cords with everyone and everything and all events. I re-attach all of my energetic cords with everything that is whole, pure, and in resonance with Love."*

Understand That Nothing Is Linear, And We Will Always Be Going Through The Ups And Downs Of The Healing Process, But We Also Learn To Take This Journey Of Life With Grace, Embracing The Waves As Part Of The Process. We no longer judge ourselves, or others, based on how far along we think we should be, or what we think we should have already accomplished.

If this is one of your Core Programmings, watching your thoughts will be key to your transformation. Give up planning or thinking about the past. Practice Gratitude, Praying, Setting Intentions, and Cutting Cords with your thought loops. Take each day as an adventure, while still taking steps towards your goals and dreams. Let Go Of The Control Over How Something Unfolds, Or When, Or Why. Trust In Your Heart That Everything Is Happening According To The Divine Plan And In Divine Time.

EXTERNALIZATION

This Programming exists for every being who has not mastered their Inner Work. The mind itself can only externalize – seeing itself would mean it's aware of itself, which it cannot be because Awareness is Consciousness. The EGO hides to protect itself, to keep your Awareness away from it so as not to dissolve it. To keep you distracted then, the EGO keeps you focused on the external.

Externalization means that we view everything as outside of us; we cannot see that everything is actually a reflection of ourselves. This creates blame, projection, anger, control, and victim consciousness. Anything that triggers us in another person, or in an experience, is because we have an unhealed part of ourselves. The sooner we accept that, the faster our transformation. Anything In The World That We Do Not Like, We Must First Take Accountability For How Our Unconsciousness Helped Create It, And How We Have Enabled Or Contributed To Its Manifestation. Then, We Focus On What We CAN Change, Within Ourself, To Heal From It.

To fully dissolve this Programming, focus on completely detaching from the external. Take Accountability for everything outside of you that triggers you, and pull all the focus onto your internal self. Heal yourself, transform your triggers, and change your own thoughts, habits, and behaviors. At the same time, hold Compassion for others and their situations, without judging them, continuing to lead by example, rather than trying to change the external circumstances.

PRINCESS/PRINCE CONDITIONING

This Programming is very prevalent within the lower feminine. This pattern of behavior is often passed down from the Earth Mother, and then enabled by parents. The Dark created the Princess Programming to convince the feminine that they are damsels in distress, needing a masculine to save them. We have taught the feminine to be spoiled, entitled, demanding, and co-dependent.

Princess Programming can present itself in many different ways: resistance to physical work, entitlement to material things, always seeking a savior (or for someone to do something for you), wanting to be coddled or pampered, believing you are a prize or trophy The underlying energy of this program is lack of Self-Love and lack of Empowerment.

The difference between a Princess and a Divine Feminine is the Divine Feminine is Fully Empowered while, at the same time, it Appreciates and Allows Masculine Support, although not demanding it or relying upon it. The Princess wants to be served, whereas the Divine Feminine seeks to serve others (with Self-Love). This conditioning is most often seen in "daddy's girls".

Prince Programming works the same way, but in the masculine. This conditioning is typically seen in "momma's boys". These masculine beings believe they should be catered to, taken care of, spoiled, pampered, and put on a pedestal. Those with Prince Programming also may have resistance to physical work, often caring about their appearance and false sense of power. They wish to be served.

To dissolve this, first reflect on where you may have this conditioning and then seek to break your resistances. Notice where you are seeking to be served, rather than to serve. Dedicating yourself in service to others, while also loving yourself, will dissolve this Programming. Seek to be in Empowered Service, where you are

Grateful and Open to Receiving Gifts and Blessings, while also not seeking them out or feeling entitled to them.

If this is one of your Core Programs, the biggest transformation for you will be physical service – cleaning, building, learning how to take care of your own car, changing your own oil, cutting your own grass, chopping your own wood, etc. Learning to handle these types of tasks will be the greatest and fastest ways to transform this Programming. Then, you will focus on Service to Love, rather than Service to Self. Remember that, You Are Worthy, Not Entitled.

BITCH CONDITIONING

This conditioning is also very deep within the lower feminine collective. Bitch Conditioning is learned from and taught by our parents. The root cause of embodying the bitch energy and actions is a fear of not being Loved. It's an underlying anger/rage at people or experiences from your life. We, as a society, have glorified and even encouraged this Bitch Conditioning by teaching the feminine that this makes them "strong" or "empowered". We often hear phrases like, *"bad bitch"*, which gives the impression that this makes the feminine cool or beautiful, or strong. But yes, this is all illusionary.

The bitch energy often presents itself through sarcasm, condescending tones, superiority, and projection. You will notice those who have Bitch Conditioning are often very reactive and very defensive … because they fear rejection. They take everything personally, which is why they then lash out in Bitch Mode. It is a protective mechanism.

In contrast, the Divine Feminine speaks Truth and has Passion, but is also filled with Compassion and Empathy. She is Open, Receptive, and Centered.

To dissolve this Programming, first look at any underlying anger or rage you are carrying. *Who do you need to Forgive? Where does the anger stem from?* Focus on releasing this anger through Crying, Journaling, and Forgiving. Focus on Breathing and Feeling the

Sensations in Your Body. Feel your heart, once again. If you are triggered, take a breath and Respond, Rather Than React.

If this is one of your main Programmings, your focus will be on Loving Yourself and Speaking with Love to Others. Whenever a bitch energy comes in, catch it, cut cords with it, and instead, respond with Love. You will begin to feel your heart soften, and you will realize that Vulnerability Makes You Stronger, Not Weaker.

ASSHOLE CONDITIONING

This conditioning presents itself in the masculine through arrogance, lack of feeling, condescending tones, superiority, and lack of vulnerability. The asshole and the bitch are the same frequencies just presenting through different vessels. The roots of the Asshole are a lack of Self-Love and a fear of being rejected. Every Asshole chooses to lash out at others due to their fear that if they are Loving and Vulnerable, they will be rejected. For them, this is a safety mechanism.

An Asshole actually desires to be Loved, but he is so afraid to give Love that, he puts up barriers and walls. This is taught by parenting and environment and is further perpetuated by masculine/feminine dynamics, which encourage this behavior – teaching the feminine that a masculine who is an Asshole to them actually Loves them. While this may be true, it enables the behavior, and round and round we go.

To dissolve this Conditioning requires a deep level of feeling. First, you must recognize the behavior and Take Accountability for it, then Work To Begin Feeling More. This starts with feeling your vessel, Meaning Feeling The Sensations Within Your Body. *Do you feel any pain, tension, stiffness, etc.?* Practice sitting with yourself and just breathing deeply, in through the nose and out through the mouth. Cut Cords with any thoughts that are trying to come in. The more you breathe, the more different emotions may surface, and tension may arise. This will give you a clue as to where the blocks to your feelings are located. Most likely, they are in your Heart Chakra.

If this is one of your Core Programmings, you need to focus on Self-Love and the Nurturing of Yourself. *When is the last time you cried? When is the last time you expressed yourself vulnerably?* These are going to be your biggest transformations – to get in tune with any anger, grief, pain or hurt stored within you, to acknowledge it, release it, express it, and Heal it. Putting Your Guard Down And Opening Yourself Up To Others Will Completely Dissolve This Programming.

SEVERE IMPATIENCE

When we are Impatient, we are struggling to Surrender. Impatience stems from fear, a fear that we need to speed things up or rush because there is not enough time. We are so focused on the destination that we miss the journey. Anxiety within the body creates this severe Impatience. When we are in anxiety – rushing and forcing – we are missing the messages, the guidance, and the syncs, which can only come when we are in the Present Moment. With Impatience, we are always living in the future.

To dissolve Impatience, one must first reflect on where it is coming from. *Are you easily distracted? Are you in fear of the future? Are you feeling anxiety?* Once you can identify the underlying emotion or feeling, you can work to resolve it. To actively slow yourself down takes deep focus and discipline. But by Slowing Down, You Can Be Present, In The Moment, Which Is Where You Are Able To Feel Peace And Clarity.

If this is one of your Core Programmings, you will have to discipline yourself to Slow Down. Meditation will be your biggest transformation. For many of you, Sitting Still for 5 minutes sounds hard enough, let alone cutting out all thoughts while you're doing it. Yet, this will be where you break through. Practice once a day just Sitting Still, Cutting Cords continuously with any thought that tries to come in. Listen to music, if that helps, and just keep breathing until you arrive at the place of Stillness and Inner Peace. Hold this for as long as you can until it becomes organic for you.

EASILY DISTRACTED

By design, all Humanity is Easily Distracted. The Dark has created an addiction to distractions to prevent us from ever getting still and going within, which is always where the transformation and quantum leaps occur. We have both outer and inner distractions that we must transform.

Outer distractions include clothes, vanity, food, social media, news, Netflix, rules, tasks, bills, sports, and the list goes on … a list that's truly endless. Any moment that you are focused on anything that is outside yourself, which prevents you from hearing your own voice within or your own heart, that is a distraction. Inner distractions usually present as a constant worry, fear, anxiety, or a thought loop that keeps you in a state of distraction. So focused on this particular fear or worry, we lose the Present Moment of Now.

Transforming distraction is done by simply staying in the Present Moment. This often sounds harder than it is, although it does take Patience and Practice. To get started, be very aware of how you live your days. If you wake up, immediately starting to think about what you need to do, or you automatically jump on your phone to begin consuming messages and news, then you are already beginning with the energy of distraction. We highly recommend carving out at least 15 minutes, as soon as you wake up, to Staying Present. You can do your morning routine, but do so without thinking, without planning, without consuming anything, thus beginning your day in a more Meditative State.

Notice how often each day you have to be doing something – reading something, listening to something, talking to someone, focusing on something external. Stillness will be your greatest friend. Within your Stillness is Clarity, Wisdom and Knowing. You can access everything through your Stillness and discover who you truly are.

The Meditation Practices listed in many of the Core Programmings already discussed apply here as well. We often live in a state of distraction because there is a wound, belief system, or some unhealed energetic within us that we must face, which we can only do when we are Still and Present with Ourself in the Now.

QUITTER

A Quitter is someone who gives up every time they reach a challenging experience. They are unable to push through the un-comfortability of the situation. There Is A Balance Between Quitting And Knowing When Something Is No Longer In Resonance With You, So You Must Let It Go. The difference is that quitting stops you from ever mastering the lessons or mastering dedication. You quit before the lesson is learned. Letting something go, because you have learned the lesson and mastered patience, dedication, and consistency, means you are ready to move onto the next level.

Reflect on anything in your life in which you gave up, where you quit before the breakthrough occurred. You may notice that similar situations, people, or lessons have continued to come back around for you, just in different ways. We Can Always See What Our Higher Self Is Guiding Us To Face Because It Will Continue To Be Brought To Us, Until We Face It. Often, we quit because the un-comfortability is too much. Whatever we need to face within ourselves feels too big.

To transform this, you must commit yourself to digging deeper into your Patience, Compassion, and Self-Reflection. Often, the lesson lies within ourself. Maybe the test is Patience, so we continue to be presented with situations that are calling for Patience, yet we give up every time it starts to take too long. Maybe you wanted to try a new hobby or sport but because you weren't getting the hang of it quickly enough, or you felt you weren't improving, you gave up. This lesson may keep coming back around for you … to test your Strength and Persistence.

If this is one of your Core Programmings, you must Identify What Pattern Is Repeating Itself. Next, commit yourself to pushing through any new challenges that come your way. As soon as whatever it is feels too hard, too much, or too overwhelming, Dig Deep Into Yourself And

Commit To Making It Through The Lesson This Time. This will be where your greatest breakthrough occurs.

INCONSISTENT

Inconsistency is one of the roots of aloofness. It is a being that often cannot commit to anything, or if they do, they cannot follow through. Quitting energy ties into this as well, as the lack of discipline. Many people were never taught consistency, nor did they ever have consistency in their childhoods, so this is an inherited or taught programming. Many parents don't push their children to stay consistent with anything. They allow them to do things as they please, and they are not required to be disciplined in anything that they do.

If you were taught Inconsistency, then you are responsible for de-programming yourself. Only you can commit to Consistency. This is one of the programs that takes time and focus to transform. Be Patient with yourself, but also recognize where your EGO is constantly trying to break your Consistency. Your EGO Wants To Keep Your Energy Scattered.

To transform this, we highly recommend choosing one Spiritual Discipline that you agree to stick to for 30 days straight – the allotted amount of time that the brain needs to turn a habit into an organic behavior. For example, if taking a walk each day is your preferred discipline, then commit to doing it EVERY day for 30 days. Notice how many times your EGO tries to fight you to prevent you from completing the task. When you can observe this from a Non-Attached State, you will begin to see how the EGO works.

If this is one of your Core Programmings, focus on the 30 day challenge and then begin reflecting on other areas of your life where you are also not consistent. *Do you often miss deadlines at work, unable to complete things on time? Do you often commit to things and then flake on them, or struggle to commit to anything at all?* Focus on where you can make changes with how you spend your energy and on what or who. If you commit to something, follow through with it. If you are given a deadline, commit to honoring it.

Often, we are first Inconsistent with things we don't enjoy but then, we begin to become Inconsistent with things we do enjoy and that are good for us. Strength comes from being Consistent, even with the things we DON'T want to do, as this will then assist us with being more Consistent on the things we do genuinely want to do that fulfill us. The habit of Inconsistency has been holding us back.

It Is Often Helpful To Have An Accountability Partner. This also works for transforming a lack of follow through or lack of integrity. Have a designated person, whether that be your partner, friend, boss, family member, or neighbor, hold you Accountable and follow up with you on things you have said you are committed to doing.

COMPLAINING

Complaining is one of the lowest frequencies on the Vibrational Scale. It carries with it the underlying energies of ungratefulness, ignorance, prince/princess programming, and victim consciousness. When we are Complaining, we are basically saying, *"I don't like xyz, and I want it to change."*

We are ungrateful in that we are not honoring the lesson or the blessing that this situation or person is showing us. We think something should be a particular way, and because it's not, we are not happy. This is ignorance. We are simply not aware of all the reasons why something is the way it is. Everything Is Divinely Designed. Often princess/prince programming comes in as the part that wants someone else to fix something for us. Our EGO is so big that we are Complaining so that someone else takes care of something that is really a lesson for us! Victim consciousness can also come in as *"cry me a river"*, complaining about circumstances or a person who YOU manifested and are responsible for.

To transform this is very simple. Every time you begin to complain about something, stop yourself, breathe, and reflect on the situation.

What is it that is triggering you? What can you change within YOU so that you are no longer bothered or upset about this person or situation? If this is one of your Deepest Programmings, then look within yourself, at what you can transform or let go of, and Flip Your Attitude To Gratitude.

LAZINESS

Laziness is very common in certain parts of the world. In the US, we have two extremes: those who are addicted to doing, working, and being busy, and then those who are extremely lazy. The bigger issue is that we also have a skewed viewpoint about what Laziness is. Taking Proper Rest And Relaxation Is Not Lazy, But Rather A Necessary Part Of Our Spiritual Growth And Healing. True Laziness is the inability to begin changing.

When we are lazy, we put things off, we procrastinate, and we make excuses for why we have not yet done something or why we don't want to do a particular thing. There are different forms of Laziness.

There is Physical Laziness that occurs when someone's vessel has no energy, more than likely because it's sucking itself dry expending energy on things that don't fulfill it, which in turn, makes the person put off things they know they need to do but can't find the motivation to do.

Emotional Laziness occurs when someone lacks feeling and is unable to dedicate emotional energy to others. These are beings who are very closed off, not often giving themselves, or others, much emotional support. They're also unable to express Vulnerability. They are Emotionally Lazy and do not want to do the Inner Work to transform their wounds and triggers, so they shut down.

Mental Laziness occurs when we are too lazy to learn something ourselves, or to find an answer or solution, so we ask someone or something outside of us. We have seen this with the Disclosure Phase – so many beings are too lazy to do their own research about Disclosure, instead, they want someone to give them an answer on a silver platter … or … they just refute information without ever having done any research themselves. We often don't take the time to actually inquire about something, to learn, research, read, digest, discern, and come to our own Truth and answer inside our heart. We want solutions, and for someone else to find them for us.

Spiritual Laziness occurs when we do not dedicate the proper energy to our Spiritual Healing, Connection with Source, and the Expansion of our Consciousness. All Humans Are Souls Having A Physical Experience, Which Means Our Spiritual Selves Need Nurturing And Healing Just As Much As Our Physical And Emotional Bodies Do. This laziness creates the belief that we are separate from God and that there is nothing Divine about us or our lives. We think we are living without Sacredness.

To transform this, we must push through our resistance and laziness. The first steps will be the hardest, but you must force yourself to get moving. Whatever you have been putting off or felt like you haven't had the motivation or energy to do, JUST DO IT! Once you push through the immediate resistance, you begin to build momentum, which you can then Balance with Rest and Reflection.

If this is one of your main Progammings, setting small goals for yourself each day will assist you. If you really want to transform this, write a list of Spiritual Disciplines you are going to do each day, then make a list of all the things you need to accomplish that you have been putting off, and a list of goals you would like to reach. Write these down on a piece of paper or on your calendar and commit yourself each day to taking one step towards your goals and accomplishments. This will take effort, but you will be amazed at the amount of energy this begins to move in your life.

45 minutes per day of physical movement is also vital for anyone who is seeking to transform laziness.

COMPLACENT

Complacency stems from defeat, apathy, and the feeling of disempowerment. When we feel we have no power to change anything, no power to make our lives different or better, we become Complacent. Change is impossible for the EGO because it can only understand what it knows. It cannot understand the Unknown, only the heart can. And this is what causes us to stay in our comfort zones or to believe we have no ability to make a difference, so why try?

In one way or another, most of Humanity is caught in this Programming. We are Complacent with our lives the way they are because changing is just so hard to do. Letting Go is so hard to do. Healing is so hard to do. So … we don't try. We give up before we even begin. We are Complacent with what we feel is outside our control.

To transform this Program, WE HAVE TO MAKE A MOVE. We often stay Complacent because, even if we do have ideas or dreams, we don't know where to begin, so we just never start. WE HAVE TO JUST TAKE A STEP, ANY STEP! We have to start being comfortable with being uncomfortable. The more we embrace change and the feeling of being uncomfortable, the more freedom we will feel to keep moving forward towards our goals and dreams. When we focus on the step that is right in front of us, the next one after the one we just so bravely took, rather than staring down the whole staircase at once, we can really begin to get somewhere.

If this is one of your Core Programs, your biggest challenge will be making changes. Take stock of your life and reflect on what aspects you want to make grander. Maybe you want to have a richer spiritual life but haven't taken any steps to actually make that happen. Maybe you've dreamt about redecorating your home to fit your energy, but it seems like too big of a project to begin. Maybe it's knowing that you don't enjoy your job, but you haven't been able to take steps to find a new one. Whatever it is, identify where you want to make changes.

Next, focus on the everyday, small steps that you are going to take to make those changes. Don't focus on the finish line or the final destination, just focus on the small steps along the way. Enjoy the process and congratulate yourself for making each small step.

REACTIVE

Reaction comes from an unhealed nervous system and the reptilian brain. We can say that all EGO is technically Reactive, as it produces a programmed response or action that is an autopilot response. This can present in a few different ways.

One, are those who get extremely triggered by things. This could be a person, idea, or word that triggers something within causing you to React in anger, defensiveness, bitch/asshole mode, or arrogance. Those who are constantly triggered are always in a Reactive State. Their nervous system is essentially fried.

Reactive Programming can also present itself as one who cannot receive. When you try and talk to this person about something or point something out that they are doing that's dysfunctional, they cannot receive and immediately shut down or throw energy back at you. They may appear calm on the surface, but as soon as they feel uncomfortable, they React. This happens often with those who have low self-esteem and live under a persona. When that persona is questioned or that belief system is breached, the reaction is swift.

The key to transforming this is through the breath. Responding Versus Reacting Is The Difference Between The Reptilian Brain And The Divine Brain. As soon as we feel a trigger – anger, frustration, or defensiveness – we must breathe. We Must Calm Our Nervous System First, Before We Respond. A Calm Nervous System Versus A Fight Or Flight Nervous System Is The Difference Between Offering A Response Or Reacting.

If this is one of your Core Programmings, you have to work on Mastering Your Triggers, and this will come through Inner Work. Identifying what triggers you have and what the roots of them are will allow you to begin transforming your reactiveness. Dissolving anger and rage are also keys to transforming this EGO Program.

CULTURAL PROGRAMMING

Cultural Programming appears in every culture and in every part of the world. These are the deeply ingrained belief systems, habits and behaviors, and culture "norms" that are passed down through the DNA. Often, there are clues to these Programmings within the stereotypes we perceive around certain cultures. Although people often take these personally, they are actually quite accurate.

For example: the white culture has certain "norms", such as being educated, having a good job, getting married, and having children. There are deep, cultural belief systems about the way things should be done and in what order, and what is acceptable. In comparison, we can look at black culture and see how there are deep cultural "norms" that are different from those of the white culture – they include great, home-cooked, soul food, the Love and support of extended family, and a Love of gospel music and R&B. These different Programmings are what often spur judgments or assumptions between these two cultures.

To transform this, you must first be honest with yourself about the Cultural Programs you have. Look at your parents, grandparents, and communities and reflect upon what the cultural norms are for you. Look at how these are different from other cultures, realizing that there is no ONE way to do anything. We are all free to create the life that resonates with us. Look at where you have conformed or adopted certain belief systems based on the culture you grew up in.

If this is one of your Core Programs, you may have to laugh at yourself when you realize that you fit the exact stereotype of that culture. Laughing At Ourselves Is The Quickest Way To Transform. Then notice which of these norms or belief systems really don't resonate with your soul, rather, they were just adopted out of obligation or judgment. Work to see every single person as an individual essence and look at yourself as an individual essence. *If you had no cultural norms or expectations, who would you be? What would you Love to do? What life would you create?* Follow that.

BLOODLUST

Bloodlust often appears in the masculine but can be present in the feminine as well. This comes from a deep lack of feeling, vengeance, and animalistic tendencies. It was ingrained in the DNA to allow the masculine to become hunters, warriors, and fighters. With our fractured Consciousness, however, we created war and violence, and so our species developed Bloodlust as a way to cope.

If we look around at our TV shows, movies, and music, we will see a large glorification of violence and bloodshed. Our animalistic brain has ingrained in us that we must dominate others and even kill them in order to survive. We were always defending ourselves, protecting ourselves, and making sure that our tribe survived.

Those with this Programming may find themselves drawn to violent things, such as violent video games, violent movies, violent shows, and violent music. You may also struggle with physical violence – getting into fights, being unable to control your rage, breaking things, etc. If you have this Programming, then your biggest challenge is Feeling, Non-Reaction, and Compassion.

To transform this, one must truly see Peace as the greatest ally. Peace and Harmony are always better than violence or domination. When we see everything in life as Sacred, we renew our respect for all life. We no longer wish to see pain, suffering, or blood on this planet. This takes a lot of Healing and Inner Awareness. Focus your energy on things that are Peaceful, such as soft music, creativity, animals, children, and shows and movies based more on Love or Laughter.

SUPER EGO

Super EGO is an advanced form of EGO characterized by extreme arrogance, thinking you know better, and fantasy and racing thought loops. Most beings spend the majority of their time in Super Ego, although they are unaware of it. Super EGO presents itself mostly in those who are very educated. This is one of the biggest flips in that those who are more "educated" have greater amounts of EGO than those who are undereducated. This is because the more education we receive, the more Programming and the more 'in the mind' we become. If we look at some of the professions that require the most education, we will see where the problem lies.

For example: to become a doctor, one must memorize and learn tons of information that is based on linear thinking, the past, and analyzation. So many doctors know all about pain, illness, disease, and medications, but they know nothing about energy, emotions, or how to connect with their patients on a heart-based level. They have no Intuition, which is why they often get so many things wrong. Or look at lawyers, who spend three years focusing on analyzing a situation from one million different angles. There's always an "answer" or a debate about an answer. It's an endless loop of the mind.

The Dark convinced us that the more education we have, the smarter we are, when in fact, it is the opposite. The more education, the more in the mind we are, the more advanced our Super EGO becomes.

However, this can also present with those with no education or less education. Those with this Programming can also always think they are smarter than others, that they know better, and they have the answers. They constantly worry, analyze, and think about things in their mind, with no ability to feel their hearts or their Intuition. They are always seeking the answer to something. We see many who have psychotic breaks, where they are hearing voices or hallucinating. This is an extreme version of Super EGO. To dissolve this Programming, it takes dedication and extreme discipline with yourself.

Whenever you begin analyzing something, running it over and over again in your mind, trying to find the answer or worrying about the solution, stop and take an ice-cold shower. Cold Showers Stop The Mind Because The Body Immediately Focuses On The Shock Of The Cold. The Cold Water Also Resets The Systems, Flushing Out The Lymphatic System And Calming The Nervous System. If you are unable to take a shower at that moment, then say out loud, *"I cut cords with everyone, everything and all events."* Do this as many times as you need to until the thought loops stop.

If this is one of your Core Programmings and you often find yourself in this energy, then you need to shift your focus onto your body, its sensations, the feelings and emotions you are having, and on your breathing. Slow it down, FEEL, and let go of thinking. Anytime your mind wants to think it knows something, wants to figure something out, say out loud, *"I don't know shit."* Surrender To NOT Knowing, Because It Is Within The Not Knowing That We Know Everything.

SPIRITUAL EGO

Spiritual EGO is the fantasy version of Spirituality, where one thinks they have attained Enlightenment, when they haven't. They think they are above others and lack accountability. This appears in any religious community and/or spiritual community. These beings are in the mind, trying to understand God, spirituality, and energies. They are not feeling, they are thinking. The easiest way to spot a Spiritual EGO is that they are convinced they have no more transforming to do, that they have reached Enlightenment and have no ability to take any further accountability and reflect upon themselves.

This also presents in the information that is put out by any channeler or spiritual person. If the information holds any attachment, fantasy, or feels or seems complex, then it is Spiritual EGO.

Love And 5D Is Very Simple. There Is Nothing Complicated About It.

We see this also in areas such as Quantum Physics. Quantum Physics is the cross between science and spirituality, however, it is based in the mind. It is trying to rationalize and find a linear thread that explains everything. True Reality Is So Multidimensional, It Can Only Be Felt And Understood Through The Heart, In A Simple Way.

To transform this, we must remember that no matter how much we "know" or how much work we've done, there are always more levels to expand into. Our work is never truly done, and as long as we are here on Earth, we will constantly be transforming until the entire planet ascends into a higher dimension. The higher the level we reach in terms of Consciousness, the greater levels of Accountability, Reflection, and Letting Go of Belief Systems need to occur.

CHAPTER TWENTY-TWO: EMBODYING THE DIVINE TRAITS

The Divine Traits are the aspects and qualities of God/Source. We are all aspects of Source and thus, by Divine Design, we embody these qualities as part of our Higher Self. These Divine Traits are essential to understand, implement, and anchor in as part of our Self-Love and Ascension Journey. Once we grasp the Programmings of the EGO and have worked to dissolve them, the Divine Traits come in for embodiment.

Utilize this guide as you are going through your journey, actively reflecting and contemplating on these traits, then allowing them to come into their full embodiment. These traits are especially useful when doing I AM Affirmations (the Mirror Technique) and can also be included in Ceremonies and Healing Work.

ACCOUNTABILITY

Most beings confuse Accountability with blame and/or punishment. When we say, *"who is accountable for this?"*, what we are really asking in our 3D way is, "who is to blame for this?". Divine Accountability, however, is quite the opposite. Divine Accountability means that we are willing to own and take responsibility for not only ourselves (and our actions) but the whole as well. When we do this, we actually dissolve our karmic energy of blame, projection, denial and deflection. We come face to face with everything that may make us feel guilt or shame, and We Own It, We Transform It, And We Heal It.

When ALL Humanity takes Accountability for all the dysfunction on the planet, that is when we will make a Quantum Leap. A Divine Being's role is to lead by example, which means we must be the first to Take Accountability for EVERYTHING. This includes the experiences we have created for ourselves, the realities we have manifested, the lessons and blessings we have chosen, and the enabling of all planetary dysfunction. When one Takes Full Accountability, they begin transforming for the entire Collective, which has an extraordinary impact on the evolutionary process. It dissolves all karmic energy being held in one's vessel, thus clearing personal karma.

Whenever we state, *"I take full accountability ... but",* we nullify the Accountability. The "but" returns us to projection and blame. One knows when Full Accountability has been taken because there is a Statement of Accountability along with an Action of Change.

UNCONDITIONAL LOVE

This planet has never experienced Unconditional Love while in the separation experiment. However, Unconditional Love Is All That Is Present In The Rest Of Creation. Many confuse Unconditional Love with enabling. Unconditional Love has Boundaries, Integrity, Self-Love, and Non-Attachment. When we look at what we have been taught as "Love", we see there are all sorts of conditions that have been placed upon it.

In our family dynamics, we Love out of obligation or guilt, and we often associate Love with doing what a family member wants us to do. In relationships, we associate Love with gifts, with someone making us feel good, or who is supporting us financially. In friendships, we associate Love with others agreeing with us, validating our opinions, and enabling our lower behavior. All of this is dysfunctional.

THE TRUE MEANING OF UNCONDITIONAL LOVE IS TO LOVE ANOTHER REGARDLESS OF THEIR CHOICES, REGARDLESS OF THEIR ACTIONS, AND REGARDLESS OF YOUR EXPECTATIONS.

We can Unconditionally Love someone and still choose to Set Boundaries, to not interact with them, or not be physically present in their lives. None of this takes away from the Unconditional Love we hold for them, yet we still Honor our Own Boundaries and Self-Love. In order to Unconditionally Love another, you must first Unconditionally Love yourself, which is why Humanity is unable to provide this Pure Love.

Unconditional Love does not control others, it does not have expectations of others, nor does it take what others do or say personally. It is Non-Attached to others' journeys, choosing to focus on the highest aspect of another being while Holding Space, Support, and Compassion for that being and their journey. Unconditional Love also knows when to provide Tough Love.

Once you have learned to unconditionally Love yourself, without judgment, shame, guilt, and repression, you will have the ability to share this Love with others in a balanced and functional way.

GRATITUDE

Gratitude is one of the most powerful energies in the Universe, as it is the basis for all Love and Manifestation. Gratitude requires one to look at the Higher Perspective of all things, to see the big picture. The Truth Is That No Matter How Low Or Dark An Experience Is, There Is Always A Lesson And A Blessing Beneath Its Surface. A true Divine Being is always Grateful for both the highs and the lows, as they both provide Growth, Expansion, and Learning. Gratitude Allows Us To Find The Purpose Within Pain And The Grace Within Suffering.

Gratitude is also the strongest force to assist with Manifestation. When we are entitled or in expectation of something, we actually push away what we want because entitlement/expectation are forceful energies, whereas Gratitude is a receptive, feminine energy.

When We Practice Gratitude Daily, We Create Space For Receptivity To Manifest Miracles, Joy, Surprises And Blessings. Even when we are not feeling the energy of Gratitude, we can practice the art of saying *"thank you"* to every person and experience that comes into our lives, especially the hard and painful ones. Gratitude Journaling also helps anchor in this energy and refocuses us on the blessings we have in our lives. The more we focus on the Blessings, rather than the lack or the challenges, the more Blessings we will attract.

WORTHINESS

Worthiness is intertwined with Gratitude. Many may mistake Worthiness for entitlement, but there is a fine line between them – the difference being Gratitude. When we are entitled, we expect something because we feel we have earned it or we deserve it. There is no Gratitude for it. When we are Grateful and hold the knowing that we are Worthy of all Love is, we allow ourselves to step into the true energy of Worthiness.

The greatest challenge is transforming our Unworthiness, as we have been programmed for thousands of years to believe that we do not deserve Grandness, Abundance, Love or Joy. We have been brainwashed to believe we must take from others or "work harder" in order to have a wonderful experience of life. We have also been programmed to believe that any mistakes we have made as humans are to be held against us, making us no longer Worthy of anything good because we have done something "bad". This causes us to accept abuse, mistreatment, and lack as normal parts of our lives.

When transforming unworthiness, it is important to understand that ALL BEINGS ARE WORTHY OF ALL THAT LOVE IS – JOY, ABUNDANCE, CONNECTION, SUPPORT, LOVE, AND MIRACLES. There is no "mistake" that can be made as a human being that can ever deprive us of this Truth.

The key is to recognize where we have not acted in Love, where we have acted from a lower place and to then transform it, which aligns us with the Worthiness that we hold.

For example: one may understand that they are Worthy of a loving supportive partner, but do not act as a loving and supportive partner themselves. They are not aligning with the energy of Worthiness because they are expecting and feeling entitled to something that they themselves are not willing to give or embody. Worthiness Equals Being Willing To Receive Exactly What Is Given Out. When we embody Unconditional Love, Grandness, Kindness, Courage, and Strength, then we know we are Worthy of Receiving that back … and we will not accept anything less.

COURAGE

Courage is a word we often associate with warriors, military, and those in battle. We say they have Courage and Strength to put themselves in harm's way. Although there is a strong element of the Warrior Energy within Courage and the Divine Masculine Energy, Courage also presents itself in many other forms. Courage means that we have the Unconditional Trust to Take a Leap of Faith. Taking Leaps of Faith means that we jump without hesitation, planning, worrying, or control. We have Courage in ourselves and the Divine, knowing that every act done in Pure Love is filled with Source.

In our daily lives, Courage presents in every decision we make. Every time we choose Love over fear, we are embodying Courage. Examples are when we choose to speak up and share our Truth, even in the face of opposition or persecution … that is Courage. When we choose to go down the unbeaten path … that is Courage. When we make decisions with our hearts instead of our minds … that is Courage. When we choose to go outside our comfort zones rather than staying boxed in … that is Courage.

The Quickest Way To Embody Courage Is To Choose Love Over Fear, Every Time. Whatever you are resistant to, afraid of, or uncomfortable doing, that is where you require Courage. When we hide our Truth or who we really are, we require Courage. We must anchor in Divine Masculine Energy and know that the Universe always supports our Boldness and Leaps of Faith.

NURTURING

Nurture is a word often associated with mothers or the feminine energy, however, all beings must anchor in the Nurturing Energy of their Divine Feminine. To be Nurturing is to be Gentle, Loving and Compassionate. Most of us were never taught how to be Nurturing, either with ourselves or others. We were taught the masculine energy of force, discipline, "do more", and "work harder".

First, We Must Be Nurturing With Ourselves. This means we must be Conscious of the ways we speak to ourselves, and the cells in our bodies. We must be Soft, Accepting, and Hold Space for ourselves, even when we fall into lower frequencies and behaviors. Next, We Must Learn How To Nurture Others. This is when we focus on our Higher Self and the Higher of Others. We acknowledge the lower, call it out as needed, and Set Boundaries. Yet, we Hold Space, we send Love, we Encourage, and we Support.

Nurturing Practices include things like Mirror Affirmations, Taking Rest when needed, Bath/Shower Meditations, creating Soft Spaces, and Taking Care of the Body.

ORGANIC

Being Organic is our natural state. Organic means we are in flow with the Universal Rhythm, and in the Present Moment of Now. Organic also means that we operate as our True Divine Selves – we do not censor or filter ourselves based on a need for validation, the fear of judgment, or because of any belief systems. When one is Organic, they are Open, Transparent, and Fully Expressive.

Our Programming, however, has taught us to be inorganic. 90% of our sense of self has been inorganic. This expresses itself through our rigid and linear behaviors and our constructed ways of speaking, dressing, and presenting ourselves.

You will know when you are in an Organic Space because you will no longer be concerned about the way other people see you, and you will no longer take actions that are based in linear or logical thinking.

An example of an Organic Being is one who Fully Loves and Accepts Themselves as they are, and who lives their daily lives as One Who Ebbs and Flows With The Natural Energies coming in. Your Full Authentic Self is then able to express!

COMPASSION

Compassion is a key trait for all human beings. The Art of Compassion is understanding its dual nature. Compassion can be Soft, Understanding, and Kind, but it can also be Direct, Assertive, and Uncomfortably Truthful. In each moment, we must *discern* which mode of Compassion is highest for ourselves and others. At the same time, in order to have Compassion for others, we must first have it for ourselves. Again, we have learned how to be hard on ourselves, no matter what. Kindness of Heart is how we Heal.

When another person triggers us or does/says something that creates an emotional reaction within us, we must not take it personal. Instead, we take a moment and recognize that those who hurt others, intentionally or unintentionally, are hurt themselves. DAMAGED PEOPLE DAMAGE OTHERS. WE MUST HOLD COMPASSION FOR THEM. Even The Darkest Beings On This Planet, We Must Hold Compassion For, As They Are Devoid Of Love, And That Is A Very Painful Experience.

However, there are moments, when the most Compassionate thing we can do for another is to tell them the harsh Truth. When we hold

Compassion for another, we understand where they are at, yet we also understand that they alone have the power to get themselves to a higher place.

Some moments call for Soft Compassion, while others call for very direct Truth to be spoken. Other times, Compassion will even call for us to create strong boundaries or to cut a person or energy from our life, so that they may learn to transform on their own. This is true Compassion.

EMPATHY

Empathy differs from Compassion in that it comes from a place of knowing (and feeling) how another feels. Compassion is an understanding, a holding of space for where another is at. Empathy comes from life experiences and can only be gained when you yourself have walked through the fires of initiation, taken on the challenges and tests, and can now Hold Empathy for another walking the same path. Many in Humanity cannot hold Empathy because they have never allowed themselves to walk this path nor open their hearts enough to know how to feel into what others are feeling.

Empathy is required as a Divine Being because it is through Empathy that we teach others. It is through Empathy that we transform pain and suffering into Wisdom and Strength. When we lack Empathy, it is because we lack the experience that another is having. We feel disconnected from their experience and thus, we cannot feel what they are feeling. This is largely the issue amongst all Humanity.

We can, in Truth, Anchor Empathy, even when we do not share the experience of another, by having our feeling centers fully turned on, allowing us to feel what another is feeling and holding space for them. This is what is occurring *when we refer to someone as an Empath – they are highly skilled at truly feeling into what another being is feeling.*

CONSISTENCY

Consistency is an essential Divine Trait for anyone on the Ascension Path and Journey, and it is much different from a routine or habit. Routines are based on auto-pilot – we do the same things, at the same time, every day. This is our typical 9-5 human experience. And we are not fully present. We are just programmed to do things, so we do them. Consistency, on the other hand, requires Conscious Dedication and Follow Through, doing what we say we are going to do.

When one says they are going to do something, or commits to a change, but cannot follow through on it, they lack consistency. When one is unable to be present and be dedicated to the moment or task, they lack consistency.

Examples are as follows: Many make New Year's Resolutions but cannot stick to them, because they lack consistency. Beings in relationships often commit to making changes, such as having better communication with their partner or committing to take certain actions, but yet they cannot sustain these changes, because they lack consistency.

Lack of consistency is a deep part of the EGO-Programmed Mind that must be dissolved.

When one is Consistent, they are committed and dedicated to their path, their craft, and their evolution. No matter what actions, disciplines, projects or changes they are committed to, They Follow Through, No Matter What. For example, if one is committed to their Spiritual Practices, they do not have to do them at the same time every day, or perform them in the same way, but they make sure they do them at the right moment and when it's highest.

A Divine Being Always Follows Through On Something They Commit To.

INTEGRITY

Integrity is a misconstrued word within the Collective. Many associate Integrity with following rules or religious doctrines. But Integrity actually means Aligning with One's Values. When one is Aligned in Integrity, their actions match their words, their outer representation matches their inner representation. One also does not compromise their Inner Values and Inner Integrity based on external circumstances.

Many in the Collective may think they are full of Integrity, yet if their external circumstances were to change, their behavior would change. Examples include those who compromise their values for money, sex, fame, or success. Also, those who say one thing but do another.

Integrity Must Be Anchored In Within The Self, First. You must get in touch with what your Core Values are and ensure that you always honor yourself, your values, your guidance, and your dreams, never compromising these for any external force.

JOY

Joy is our innate state of being. When we are in our natural state, we are Full of Joy. Joy does not mean we will never experience pain or sadness, yet it means that we have a foundation of Joy to always bring us back to a focus on the Higher Perspective. Joy comes from within and can never be developed by anything external. When we make our Joy and Happiness dependent on people, money, jobs, friends, or circumstances, we give away our power to those things. This sets us up for disappointment, attachment, and depression.

To cultivate an Inner Sense of Joy, one simply has to focus on the Higher Perspective within all things. Even when we are presented with challenges, tests, loss, or sadness, we must always look to what we are being taught, the gift and silver lining that is being shown to us. Even in the darkest of times, we can find Joy, when we focus on what is beautiful about our experience.

Focus on what you DO have, which is always Love, Connection, and Community. Be Grateful for everything in your life and Find Joy In The Small Things, The Simple Things. Our Truest Joy Comes From Simply Being Present With Life And Appreciating Its Profound Beauty.

TOLERANCE

Tolerance is the Divine Trait of Accepting Others no matter how different or contrary they appear to you. Our world today lacks tolerance, as everyone seeks to impose their beliefs, opinions, and perspectives onto others. This is an assault on Sovereignty and stems from deep arrogance. When we are Tolerant of others, we allow them to be as they are. We do not seek to change them, convince them, or save them in any way. Instead, we Tolerate their differences.

When we can embody Tolerance, we Allow Space for others to discover their own path. ALL of Humanity has the same destination, but we have very different paths to getting there. When we try and control another's path, we are actually taking them away from their destiny. Therefore, when we embody Tolerance, we are embodying Non-Attachment as well.

PURE THOUGHT

Pure Thought simply means that you keep your thoughts in the Higher. Any thought that does not bring you Joy is of the EGO-Programmed Mind. As soon as a lower thought enters, use your tools of Cutting Cords And Replace It With A Higher Thought. When one is pure of thought, they generate no karma, and they also become a lighthouse of energy.

Lower thought, or the EGO Mind, is what creates all dysfunction on the planet. Thoughts create reality, and when 8 billion people are in lower thought, we create Hell. When we are in Pure Thought, we are assisting with creating the New Earth, rather than feeding the lower paradigm.

If you struggle to keep your thoughts in the Higher, then more Inner Work is needed, specifically around judgement.

RECEPTIVE

Receptivity is a Divine Feminine Trait which we all must anchor within. When we are Receptive, we do not have walls around our hearts, we are open. Being Receptive, however, does not mean we do not have boundaries. We Are Able To Receive And Then Discern. This process works in our daily life in every interaction we have. Remember that life is always interacting with us, and part of Receptivity is Being Open to Receiving Messages From All Places. If you lack receptivity, you will be combative, resistant, and closed off.

For example: most beings do not notice the Synchronistic Signs of the Universe because they are not open and receptive to seeing them. We are taught we must strive, seek, and force things to come to us, including Love, Abundance, Stability and Joy. This actually creates a wall that prevents us from being a match to receiving these things.

When we are Receptive, we receive (in our auric fields) information, communication, signs, and experiences, and we do not try to fight against or block anything coming through. Then, from these interactions, We Discern What Resonates With Us. We Keep What Resonates, And We Discard The Rest.

PATIENCE

Patience is one of the most important Divine Traits. On this Journey of Ascension, we must be Patient with ourselves, others, and the process. In Truth, everything is happening simultaneously and also in Divine Time. When we lack patience, we often try and force things to happen before they are Divinely Timed to occur, thus working against Creation.

Patience does not mean lack of action, yet it works with Divinely-Inspired Action. When we feel into taking an action, and then wait to see if our Intuition is in alignment with this action, allowing the energy of said action to unfold and be recognized, then we have embodied Patience. We Are Allowing The Space For Things To Unfold Organically And Perfectly.

If you lack patience, Get In Tune With Your Feeling Centers And Intuition, so that you will always know when the proper time is to act. *Rule of thumb: don't act when you don't know, act when you know.* Your knowing will give you the proper timing.

TRANSPARENT

Transparency is key. Many believe Transparency means they must disclose or share every single detail or piece of information. However, the true meaning of Transparency is to see no difference between you and the outside world. There is no barrier between the internal and the external. When we remove this barrier, we understand that everything outside of ourselves is a reflection of us on the inside, thus changing the way we interact with the world.

When one is Transparent, they find no need to lie, manipulate, hide, or "beat around the bush." They understand that everything is a reflection of themselves, therefore, to lie to or hide from another is to lie to and hide from oneself.

As we develop Divine Transparency, we will find that we no longer fear judgment and rejection. We are Fully Authentic, Truthful and Open.

SELF-LOVE

A DIVINE BEING HAS FULL SELF-LOVE, BECAUSE IN ORDER TO LOVE ANOTHER, YOU MUST FIRST LOVE YOURSELF.

Humanity lacks Self-Love, which is why they are incapable of Unconditional Love. We are taught to judge and criticize ourselves, never accepting ourselves as we are. Self-Love is the most important aspect one can anchor in, and it supports all of the other Divine Traits.

To anchor in Self-Love fully, one must not only change the way you speak and look at yourself, but you must also be disciplined in building Self-Love Routines into your everyday life. Self-Love Disciplines, such as Mirror Affirmations, Journaling, Movement, Singing/Dancing, Nurturing and Self-Care, are all essential to anchoring in Self-Love.

Look at where you cast judgment, shame, blame, and unworthiness onto yourself and begin to change your communication. Remember that the thoughts we think and the words we speak to ourselves are heard by our cells, and our body then reflects the amount of Self-Love it is given.

BEAUTY

Beauty is often seen as how we appear externally, yet true Divine Beauty is within. When one embodies Beauty, they not only see themselves as the beautiful Divine Being they are, but they also hold this perspective of everyone and everything. One who embodies this trait sees the Beauty within all life, nature, and other beings, holding them all to be Sacred.

If you lack beauty, then you lack Self-Love. Focus on identifying all things that are beautiful about you internally, and then begin to focus on the beauty of everyone and everything. We can always appreciate external beauty as well, such as making a beautiful home and space for ourselves, taking care of our things, and appreciating the beauty of life. In addition, we also must focus on the beauty of the energy around us, the spirit within all things.

KINDNESS

Being Kind and being nice are very different. "Nice" refers to being fake, which enables others. One who seeks to be nice cares only about how they are externally perceived. They put on a show of being "nice", yet there is no depth behind it. Being Kind is being Pure of Heart, showing Compassion, Empathy, and Care for Others.

When we embody Kindness, we choose to Love others and Be in Service to the Whole. This does not mean we will always be perceived as "nice", yet we are Kind, meaning our Intentions are pure and our actions are always for the Highest Good of ourselves and others.

For example: A friend asks us for a favor which we do not really want to do. The nice person says, *"okay I'll do it!"*, but their action is filled with resentment because they do not actually wish to do this favor. They are just seeking to be "nice." The Kind person feels into why they do not want to do this favor. *Is there resistance? Maybe the favor isn't rooted in equal energy exchange.* Once the Kind person has reconciled within, they may say, *"I'm sorry I am not able to do that favor for you, but I am here to support you in any other way I can. I will make a few calls and see if anyone can assist."* Here, The Action Is Pure Of Heart And Personal Boundaries Have Been Respected, even though the response is the opposite of that of the nice person.

CHILDLIKE WONDER

Childlike Wonder exists within us all! We are all born with this wonder of the world, an excitement for life, and a general Sense of Joy. This is slowly stripped from us as we mature, though, as the 3D world forces upon us obligations, guilt, stress and lack. We stop doing things for Pure Joy and instead, we do things because we have to.

As we continue on this Journey of Healing and Evolution, we must regain our Childlike Wonder. This is the perspective of seeing everything as a Miracle and a Blessing, always being Open to Learning Something New. We no longer see everything as a negative or an obligation. We don't hold a rigid sense of what we think we know. This allows Pure Imagination and Joy to fill us, and life once again returns to Fun and Adventure.

BRILLIANCE

Every being in Creation is Brilliant, for they have been created by Source, the most Brilliant Being of All. We can see Brilliance like a diamond showing the colors of the rainbow in all its many facets and angles. When a diamond shines, it shines in all directions, creating Brilliance. This is what we must get in touch with – our Multi-Dimensional Selves.

The 3D world taught us that we must only be one thing – our identity. That identity is normally constructed around our family, our gender, our job, and our titles. For instance, many parents construct their entire identity around being a parent. That is who they are. Many others also construct their identity around their job. *"I am a doctor" or "I am a builder"*. And they never expand beyond that identity.

As Multi-Dimensional Beings, we were never created to just be one thing. When we allow all aspects, sides, and parts of ourselves to be

Loved, Recognized, and Given the Opportunity to Express, we embody our true Brilliance.

PURITY

Purity is not the same as the false religious purity that has been programmed into the masses. This false version of purity created judgment and shame, especially around sexual energy and relationships. True Divine Purity means Energetic Purity. When one is Energetically Pure, they have done the inner transformation and dissolved their lower aspects. They embody pure thought and are now a pure energetic vessel.

When one is Pure Energetically, they naturally and organically purify all lower behaviors and actions that are typically viewed as dysfunctions. For instance: one who is pure energetically could take an action that is exactly the same as one who is not energetically pure, and the outcome of that action will be completely different. The Energetically Pure Being will gain Blessings due to their Pure Intention, while the one who is not energetically pure will often gain a lesson or additional karma.

DIVINE WISDOM

Divine Wisdom can only be found through experience. 3D wisdom is based off of Programming and intellectual study, often just taking the advice of others. Many teach things they have never experienced themselves or experiences that they have not learned the lessons of and as a result, evolved to the Higher.

For example: one may have experienced abuse in their life, and now they are offering wisdom to others who are experiencing the same. However, the teacher has never transformed their own wounds resulting from the abuse they suffered, such as victim consciousness, blame, projection, resentment, guilt, shame, fear, or lack of trust. Thus, their teachings are not based on True Wisdom.

True Divine Wisdom comes from walking your talk, embracing every experience, finding the blessing within it, and most importantly, transforming all the lower energies of that experience. This is the true path of wisdom and sharing wisdom with others. Wisdom does not come from intellect, study or listening to others. It comes purely from your own *knowing*.

RESPONSIVE

LOVE ALWAYS RESPONDS; IT NEVER REACTS. Being Responsive requires you to not take anything personally. When we take something personally, it becomes a trigger. When we have failed to transform a wound, then any external action, word, or experience can cause us to be triggered. This is where reaction comes from – being unhealed.

When we are Healed and do not take things personally, it allows us to be responsive rather than reactive. This means that we are Centered and Balanced within our response, and we are not coming from a triggered place. Responsiveness also means that we respond to all of life. We do not ignore what we don't like or prefer. When we have a Synchronicity or sign shown to us, we Respond to it. We are Grateful, Reflective, and we Apply It.

PERSERVERANCE

Perseverance is a Divine Masculine Trait that we all must embody. When we face tests and challenges, and we persevere through them, we then get the Blessing. What often happens with those in the EGO-

Programmed Mind is that they give up before the Blessing comes. When things get hard, when they are required to change, or when the tests are challenging, they quit before the Lesson is learned.

Remember that every test and challenge that we receive is orchestrated by our Higher Self for our growth and evolution. When we do not learn the Lesson of the test, we then must repeat it. This is why many seem to have the same experiences over and over again – they have not learned to persevere through the storm to arrive at the rainbow.

INNER STRENGTH

Inner Strength comes from knowing ourself, loving ourself, and creating a strong inner foundation. This is done through Inner Work, Self-Love Practices, and a Deep Unconditional Trust in the Self and the Divine. When we lack Inner Strength, we are unable to be courageous or face the tests and challenges.

Inner Strength is often associated with a disconnection from emotion. One is seen as "strong" internally when they are not emotional or deep feeling, but this is a false sense of Inner Strength. It takes a much deeper level of Inner Strength to be able to feel all our feelings, and then still move forward with Courage and Bravery. To be able to transmute all of the sadness and grief and still have the strength to keep going. This is the Divine Warrior Energy.

Develop your Inner Strength through Compassion, Trust, Self-Love, Forgiveness and Purpose. When You Stay Focused On Your Purpose, Your Inner Strength Follows.

ABUNDANT

Abundance is an energy, not a possession or specific item. We often associate Abundance with money, but Abundance comes in ALL forms. When we are in our Divine State, we are naturally Abundant because Source is limitless and eternal. There is no such thing as lack in Creation.

As we transform our lack consciousness and fear, we begin to feel this energy of Abundance within. Being Abundant means we focus on all of the Blessings we DO have, we hold Gratitude for them, and we also know we are Worthy of Grandness. One cannot manifest Abundance if they are not Abundant in Spirit, Love, Gratefulness, and Compassion. When we look at Abundance as an energy, we will see that we must also Create Space for it to enter our lives.

Every time our mind seeks to focus on what we are lacking, or need more of, we must refocus on what we already have. The true nature of being Abundant is that everything is provided in the moment it is needed, no more and no less.

Practice the Abundant Embodiment by noticing how Source provides you with exactly what is needed in every moment, even if that means a Lesson instead of a Blessing.

DIVINE INTUITION

Divine Intuition is a Divine Trait of the Feminine that we all hold within. Our Divine Intuition comes from our feeling centers, our Intuitive knowing, and our heart connection. When we are embodying our Divine Intuition, we are not only listening to our hearts and our inner knowing, but we are also acting upon them.

Many beings have developed a strong Intuition but fail to act on it. Their minds make them doubt or second guess their Intuition, which leads to a blockage. In order to have our Divine Intuition fully embodied, we must follow our pings, no matter where they lead us. There is never a wrong choice, there is only learning and living.

To activate your full Divine Intuition, talk to your Angels, follow your pings, notice the signs and Synchronicities. And when you are acting upon your Divine Intuition, you will receive Confirms that you are on the right path.

DIVINE INTELLIGENCE

Divine Intelligence is far beyond the 3D intelligence that many seek. 3D logical intelligence is born of the mind and the left brain. It follows logical and linear patterns, and it is unable to access the Divine Intelligence of Source, which follows no logical or linear path. Divine Intelligence is activated via our right brain as well as our Crown Chakra.

Focusing on the activation of the right brain will allow more Divine Intelligence to flow through you, as well as dissolving any attachments you have to belief systems, logic, and linear thinking. Divine Intelligence is a perfect combination between the brain and heart – the brain is able to decode the information, and the heart is able to provide Intuitive knowing.

When one is embodying Divine Intelligence, they are able to see beyond the surface level and instead make decisions and choices based on Intuition as well as Understanding. Others will often not understand your behavior patterns or why you choose certain actions, but your Divine Intelligence knows what is in your best interest.

Our vessels also naturally hold this Divine Intelligence, which means our cells are always communicating to us, and we are responding.

TENACITY

Tenacity is our Divine Masculine Grit. When we embody Tenacity, we have the capacity to make it through any test or challenge because we refuse to give up. A Divine Being keeps going, no matter what. This does not mean we force or push ourselves, or deny Self-Love, but we possess the Tenacity of Source within us to master all things that are thrown our way.

When we lack tenacity, we tend to choose the easy route, or the safe route. The challenging path requires Tenacity and Stamina of Spirit, which most humans lack. This prevents us from reaching our highest potential, our grandest version of Self.

The Path of Ascension requires Grit, the Tenacity to push forward at all costs because we understand the importance each of us hold. No Matter How Challenging The Path Appears To Be, Remember That You Are Strong Enough To Walk It.

SELFLESSNESS

Selflessness is also a key trait of the Divine. This does not mean that we abandon ourselves or put others above ourself, rather, it means that our actions and choices are always focused on the Highest Good of all. This is Pure Selflessness. Most of Humanity makes choices based on what will benefit them the most, what will satisfy their EGO wants, needs, and desires. They are not making choices that would serve the whole.

When we are truly Selfless, we understand that the whole is always more important than the individual. Again, this does not mean we put ourselves in the corner or that we lack Self-Love, we simply understand that Unity Consciousness is far more grand than individual separation.

In every action you take, ask yourself if this is benefitting the whole or not. The best example of this is those who choose to dedicate their life in service to Humanity over personal gain. This is true and Pure Selflessness in action. When we give to others without expectation or the need for a return, that is Divine Selflessness. Also, when we act in Self-Love, we are benefiting the whole.

PASSION

Passion is the Divine Masculine Trait that is the sister energy of Compassion. Passion is often seen as "anger" to those who are living in the mind, yet it holds an entirely different frequency. Our Passion is our life force; it is the pure spark of life force energy that is expressed through our Inspiration, Convictions, and Encouragement. Our Passion inspires others, and it is a necessary component of our journey. Without Passion, we are passive, lifeless, and docile.

Many lack passion because they see it as "anger", which has become socially unacceptable, and so they suppress their passion and become weak. Passion is our driving force. It is our Love of Life, God, and Humanity. Our Passion is what brings the fire of life into our bones and sparks it in others.

To know the difference between anger and Passion, simply look at your frequency. If you are taking something personally and are triggered and resentful, then anger can come through. If you are Centered, Balanced, and Harnessing Your Inner Strength, your Passion will be able to come through.

Our Passion Is Also What Gives Us The Fire To Follow Our Dreams, To Do What Brings Us Joy, And To Fight For Love.

DIVINE WILLPOWER

Willpower is a Divine Trait that sounds similar to Tenacity and Dedication, but it differs in one key way – when we are Dedicated, we are able to stay committed to what we have set out to do, and we are consistent with our efforts; when we have Tenacity, we have the inner strength to keep going through tests and challenges; Willpower, however, comes from our Unbreakable Connection with Source. The words *will + power* have often been associated with one who exerts their power in order to meet their own will, but Divine Willpower is when we use our power solely for the purpose of Divine Will.

Example: A being who has an incredible will to build their own business and become successful will use all their power to achieve this goal. However, if you were to present to this same being the idea for them to build a service-based business that would not make them monetarily successful, but would have a major impact on the world, they would probably choose not to do it, because their will power was coming from Self, not the Divine.

Divine Willpower allows us to act from our power source, our Solar Plexus. It allows us to believe in ourself, that we are capable of achieving impossible things utilizing our power for Divine Will, rather than for Self Will. Divine Willpower will carry you through to accomplishing things that you never imagined, simply because the Divine is backing you. It is the Divine use of Power.

HONOR

Honor is a word we often associate with a knight or soldier. These archetypes hold Honor for themselves and for what they are fighting for. We have often heard the phrase *"honor your parents"*. However, True Honor is when we not only Honor ourselves, and our own Core Values, but we are also willing to fight for those values and fight for Love.

When One Has Embodied Honor, They Honor Themselves First And Foremost. This can occur in many ways, such as Honoring Your Body by listening to its subtle messages, Honoring Your Feelings by allowing them space to be expressed, and Honoring Your own Intuition and Guidance by following it. When we Honor Another, we Honor the Higher of That Person, we Honor Life and All of Creation, holding it as Sacred. And We Are Willing To Fight And Stand Up For All That Is Love And All That Is Sacred.

TRUTH

Truth means many things to different people, but it is a Core Value that we all must embody. Truth simply means what is correct and true for us at any given moment. When we embody Truth, we Speak the Truth of Our Hearts, we are Open, Honest and Transparent, and we also are able to Discern What is Real and What is Not.

Humanity relies on "proof" and "facts" to tell them what is true and what is not. Real Truth, however, comes from the Heart and from Intuition. It does not rely on facts or proof, only the Feeling. In this way, Our Truth Can Often Change, As We Change And Evolve. As Mother used to say, *"Truth is what is highest and best in each moment"*.

We must allow Truth to Evolve, to Grow, and to Change. We must be Non-Attached to what we see as Truth (in the moment), and just Follow our Inner Knowing and our Inner Compass. When we do this, we will always be anchored in Divine Truth.

FAITH

Faith is different than Trust or Hope. Faith is the deep optimism inside of us that allows us to know that everything will always work out exactly as it should. When We Hold Faith Within Us, We See The Highest Perspective And The Highest Timeline, *Always*. We focus on the Light and the Positive, but we do not bypass the lower.

Faith gives us the ability to take 'leaps of faith' that the average person who lacks Faith is unable to take. When we shoot for the stars, we go big with our dreams, and we are embodying Faith. When we hold that Trust and Knowing inside of ourselves, we Open Up to Miracles and Limitless Possibilities. Faith brings the invisible into the visible, and it makes the impossible, possible.

TRUST

Trust is a requirement for our Divine Embodiment. Unconditional Trust Means That We Trust Love, Source, And The Universe, *At All Costs*. We also Fully Trust Ourselves. This Unconditional Trust can never be shaken, as we know that Source is always in charge and is always supporting us, no matter what. This allows us to embody the Bravery and Courage needed to walk our path.

When we lack trust, we then try and control the external, forcing or making things happen because we do not trust they will occur. We also enter linear and logical thinking, trying to work out why something happened. At our worst, we think we know better than God, and we then deviate from the Divine Plan, no longer trusting in it.

When we are rooted (Root Chakra) in Unconditional Trust, we have a solid foundation. We are Centered, Balanced and Calm. We hold the Power of the Divine Within Us, and we are unshakeable.

DIVINE EMPOWERMENT

Divine Empowerment comes from the Solar Plexus, and we embody this trait when we take our power back from external sources. We no longer seek external validation or control but are Divinely Empowered From Within. When we embody our Empowerment, we make choices and take actions based on Internal Trust.

When we are Divinely Empowered, we also do not seek to fill a void from external sources (through substances, money, sex, relationships, or success, for example). We are no longer controlled by lack or fear of the outside world. We Own Our Divine Power from Source. This allows us to Act From Love and not fear.

GRACE

Grace is the Divine Trait of Accepting, Embracing and Allowing. Grace comes through suffering, embracing all the ups and downs of the human experience. In Grace, we allow the unfoldment of life without restriction, resistance, or control. We Respond With Love rather than reacting from fear. Grace allows us to Find The Purpose Within Our Pain and to Find The Meaning Of The Web Of Events That Make Up Our Life.

In order to embody Grace, one must allow the full experiences of both the Lessons and the Blessings. When we seek only the Blessings and bypass the Lessons, we miss the opportunity to embody Grace.

Grace allows us to teach others how to walk the path of Love. It calls for Compassion and Empathy as well as Understanding and Appreciation.

LAUGHTER

Laughter is a Divine Trait that is essential to our Higher Self. As Divine Beings, we naturally embrace the comedy of existence. All of Creation holds the energy of Laughter, which is the highest expression of Joy. Laughter has the ability to Heal, to Raise Vibration, and to Dissolve Fear. Laughter has often been used in the lower to create a mask, or to cover up pain. However, when we learn to allow LAUGHTER AS THE ULTIMATE HEALING TOOL, not to take away our pain but to guide us through it, we transmute the lower into the higher.

LAUGHTER IS THE KEY TO LIFE ON THIS ASCENSION JOURNEY. No matter how challenging our life appears to be or how big the tests are, they are never more than we are capable of handling. Laughter re-hearts us that all is perfect within the Divine Design, and that the human experience is meant to bring Joy to our lives.

CHARITY

The Divine Trait of Charity is much different than the 3D understanding of it. In 3D, charity would mean giving without awareness, or giving out of pity. EGOs often want to be seen as charitable, yet they give with no Pure Intention or Love. The true Divine Nature of Charity is equal to Philanthropy, meaning We Give Selflessly, Out of Love, and With the Intention of Bringing Joy, Healing, and Support.

True Charity knows that giving to that which is dying (energetically), or that which is in a taking state, is also not true giving. Giving to a blackhole only creates more blackholes, therefore, the true nature of Charity Carries With It The Discernment Of Where Is The Highest To Give Our Energy, Love And Support To, And This Is What New Earth Is Based On.

As an example of this, many believe they appear to be "charitable" because they donate to well-known charities such as the Red Cross or a children's hospital. However, there is so much corruption and lower energetics around these "well-known" charities, that by giving to them, without Full Awareness, you have actually just participated in the taking state from which they operate. Instead, it would be much more Charitable to give to someone you meet, or know, with the Full Intention of Giving Love and Support to that person, who has Received in Gratitude. That is true Charity.

HUMILITY

Humility is the Divine Trait of knowing one's power and one's worth, while also being Humble within the knowing of that power. Those that have Humility do not seek to prove their brilliance or power to others, nor do they need validation of their worth. They hold Humility in the knowing and trusting of themselves.

Humility is Moderate, Balanced and Calm. It is not overstated, nor does it require attention from others. Humility allows us to stand tall in our Light and our Brilliance and to Shine It Outwards, *with no attachment* to those who acknowledge our Light. Without Humility, we get caught in the EGO trap of needing others to validate who we are.

DIVINE PERCEPTION

Divine Perception is Seeing Through the Eyes of God. When we hold a Divine Perception, we are able to see the Higher Perspective of all things. We see the silver lining of all experiences – that everything is either a Lesson or a Blessing.

We are also able to see all beings in their Higher, regardless of how they appear in their human form. We acknowledge the God within all things and all others, which keeps our perception in the realm of the Divine. This trait allows us to bring in Divinity through our experiences and into everyone and everything we encounter.

When we lack Divine Perception, we look at everything in the lower, and we also lack the higher ability to see beyond the surface level of our experiences and situations. This only further creates lower experiences.

FULL FEELING

Full Feeling is the Divine Trait of being Open, Receptive, and In Tune With Your Emotional Body. When we lack Full Feeling, we have blocks to our Heart Chakra and thus are unable to fully feel our emotions, express them, and feel the emotions of others.

Most of Humanity has been taught to suppress and numb their feelings because feelings are often associated with pain or uncomfortable emotions. However, this suppression and numbing only leads to a closed Heart Chakra, where we are unable to give Compassion, Empathy or Understanding to ourselves and others.

Full Feeling Requires Us To Allow ALL Emotions To Come Up, Be Felt, Expressed, And Then Cleared. No Matter How Uncomfortable The Emotion, It Must Be Acknowledged And Then Expressed. Tools and techniques for Full Feeling include Crying/Releasing, utilizing Ceremonies for Emotional Cleansing, Water Therapy, Journaling, and Divine Communication with others.

GENUINE

When we are Genuine, we express our True Nature and True Self. Humanity has been taught to put on masks, and these masks are used to hide the True Self, so that only the false or inauthentic versions of ourselves are expressed. At the root, this comes from our fear of rejection.

When we hide our True Selves, we become inauthentic, and we lack the genuine organic expression of the Divine Self. To Anchor In Our Genuine Energy, It Starts With Being Honest With Ourselves About Who We Are And What We Feel. We then express our True Feeling, True Selves, and our Personal Truths to others, regardless of whether or not our Truth is accepted by others.

By being Genuine, we will also attract other Genuine Beings, and our lives will become much more whole and enriched.

HEART-CENTERED

Being Heart-Centered means that We Lead From The Heart. This requires us to have Full Feeling and an Open Heart Chakra. The Heart is our foundation, and when we operate outside the Heart Center, we easily fall into fight or flight survival mode and linear thinking. This leads to us making decisions out of fear rather than Love.

Becoming Heart-Centered requires us to feel into actions before we take them to ensure we are not acting in fear but in Love and Knowing. Whenever we are feeling overwhelmed, triggered, or unsure of what to do, breathing consciously in through the nose and out through the mouth for a few minutes helps to bring us into our Heart Center.

NON-ATTACHED

All Divine Beings are Non-Attached to persons, places, or things. This is because a Divine Being understands that WE ARE ALL ONE, and always connected. Therefore, we can never "lose" anything, nor can we be separated from anything. The Divine Being also knows that time is eternal, and our souls are immortal, so there is no fear of not having enough time or running out of time.

To practice Non-Attachment, practice stating out loud, *"I AM not attached to any person, place, or thing."* Notice when your mind begins to go into fear about losing a person, environment, job, item, or relationship, and Practice The Art Of Letting Everything Go, working through the emotions of loss, heartbreak, fear, and lack.

PROACTIVE

A Divine Being is always Proactive in that they Take Initiative! Humanity has been taught to be lazy and procrastinate in taking actions or making changes, which leads to weakness and stagnancy. The Divine Being Takes Inspired-Action and is Proactive in Making Changes that they are being guided to make.

The key is to remember that every time we have a feeling or nudge to express something, do something, or make a certain change, our

Higher Self is communicating with us. When we ignore these messages and nudges, we shut down the connection between ourself and our Intuition and Higher Self.

By being Proactive, we are consistently moving energy forward, which leads us to greater Evolution, Blessings, and Transformation.

HUMBLE

Being Humble is similar to having Humility, but while Humility provides us with Inner Worth and Empowerment without needing validation, being Humble gives us Gratitude and Appreciation for all things. When we are Humble, we are not seeking to prove anything to anyone, nor are we looking to be put on a pedestal, We Are Simply Grateful For Our Lives, Our Experiences, And All Of Our Blessings And Lessons.

One can be Humble yet also know their own power and worth. Many people confuse being Humble with hiding one's power or having low self-esteem. This is fake humbleness and comes from a lack of Self-Love and Knowing. When we are truly Humble, we are Grateful for everything, yet we are Strong in Who We Are and in Our Sense of Worth.

CHAPTER TWENTY-THREE: SELF-LOVE DISCIPLINES

The Daily Self-Love Disciplines are a path for Higher Self Embodiment! Self-Love is how we become our greatest/grandest vision/version of ourselves. It's simple, fun, and anyone can do it!

The key is Consistency (a minimum 30 days), Embodiment, Change (both internal and external), and Soul Growth. It isn't an overnight process.

One of our Soul Purposes during this Ascension Process is to embody our Higher Self – to remember who we are as a Creation of/Fractal of Source. If you have been searching for your Soul Purpose, this is ONE of them!

Our whole lives we have been taught who to be in order to serve a system that is not designed to empower us. Our Higher Selves (Souls) have come here to Earth encoded with our purpose for the role we will play in this time. Practicing the Self-Love Disciplines, we strengthen our connection to that higher part of ourselves, activating our Inner Trust and Guidance as well as our Gifts.

The Self-Love Disciplines are here to replace low-vibrational habits with high-vibrational disciplines that will eventually lead to consistency within other aspects (i.e. service to others) of our daily life. If you know you are here to help others/Humanity, you must start the journey by taking care of yourself first. *How can you serve others from the heart if you aren't giving Self-Love to yourself first?*

You must start the journey from within, simply because that is how energy works. Our ideas lead to action; in other words, our Inner Work leads to results in our outer reality.

Daily Consistency is key to creating amazing results in our lives. The Intention behind each of the Disciplines will create an equal experience in your external world. *So within, so without.* The more you tend to the garden within, the more your external world will mirror that back to you. With Daily Practice, these Disciplines and Tools will become a part of how you interact with others, how you speak to and show up in the world. They are incredible Tools for Transformation.

When you do your Self-Love Disciplines, Be in the Present Moment … in the Moment of Now. It's not about doing them all just to say you did them, it is meant to be a Healing Experience. If you would like to choose some Disciplines and not all of them to start out, that is okay. If you would like to do them all, that's wonderful (and it's also our recommendation as well)! This is due to the fact that this will lead to the highest soul growth possible. Regardless, follow the path your soul is creating for you.

The Disciplines are for Self-Love Growth, and some or all should be done for a minimum of 30 days. They are techniques you can use in your day-to-day life, whenever you feel guided to do so. As you do them more consistently, they will become natural to you. For example: The tool of Blessing Your Food is not something you should stop doing after 30 days. It's something that becomes a healthy habit over time, if you resonate with it and it works for you.

During this process, follow your Intuition. Feel the energy that comes through as you do each Discipline. Try them all out … or try out some. *The most important thing is to trust that your soul is guiding you. And have fun!* If there is anything you can give to yourself, it is the Gift of Self-Love.

The Self-Love Disciplines make a significant difference in your Inner Peace and Joy, and they are easy and fun to do. Below is a list that you can keep on a device or print out. We also have a printable checklist on our website at 5DFullDisclosure.org so you can track and check off the Disciplines and Tools you're using each day! You can begin with a few, just be consistent and then keep adding more to your day … or whatever method works best for you!

The Morning Gratitude Prayer

Good morning, Love and all the angels and all in creation! Thank you for the many blessings and Love surprises as I walk in Love with my every thought and every action. Thank you for the miracles and the magical, synchronized events, which are lighting up my life with overflowing joy.

Thank you for the laughter today and the aha moments as I remember more of the Love I truly am and share this with others. Thank you for all this energy of Love and oneness pouring into the planet and, through me, activating all that is dormant, so I may serve in the wholeness of Love. Thank you for the increased visions of Love which are assisting in the manifestations of the New Earth, where only Love exists. I am honored, I am worthy of all that Love is, and I thank Love this day for this realization in my life. Thank you, Love. Thank you, angels. I am here. I am present, and I am ready to be who I really am and to live my life in Love.

The Four Agreements by Don Miguel Ruiz

The Four Agreements, according to Bestselling Author Don Miguel Ruiz, teach that, everything we do is based on agreements we have made — agreements with ourselves, with other people, with God, and with life. But the most important agreements are the ones we make with ourselves. In these agreements, we tell ourselves who we are, how to behave, what is possible, and what is impossible. One single agreement is not much of a problem, but we have many agreements that come from fear, deplete our energy, and diminish our Self-Worth.

In *The Four Agreements*, Don Miguel reveals the source of the self-limiting agreements that rob us of joy and create needless suffering. When we are ready to change these agreements, there are four deceptively simple, yet powerful agreements that we can adopt as guiding principles. From his bestselling book of the same name: "Based on ancient Toltec wisdom, *The Four Agreements* offer a powerful code of conduct that can rapidly transform our lives to a new experience of freedom, true happiness, and Love."

Read (or say out loud to yourself) The Four Agreements at least once a day. After doing so consistently for 30 days, you can always reference them whenever you feel guided to do so as a tool to use to get back to your Heart Center. As outlined in the book, The Four Agreements are as follows:

➢ ***BE IMPECCABLE WITH YOUR WORD***

Speak with integrity. Say only what you mean. Avoid using the word to speak against yourself or to gossip about others. Use the power of your word in the direction of Truth and Love.

- ***DON'T TAKE ANYTHING PERSONALLY***

Nothing others do is because of you. What others say and do is a projection of their own reality, their own dream. When you are immune to the opinions and actions of others, you won't be the victim of needless suffering.

- ***DON'T MAKE ASSUMPTIONS***

Find the courage to ask questions and to express what you really want. Communicate with others as clearly as you can to avoid misunderstandings, sadness, and drama. With just this one agreement, you can completely transform your life.

- ***ALWAYS DO YOUR BEST***

Your best is going to change from moment to moment; it will be different when you are healthy as opposed to sick. Under any circumstance, simply do your best, and you will avoid self-judgment, self-abuse, and regret.

Sun Gazing

When you are staring at the sun, you are connecting to and accessing Source Consciousness and Universal Plasma Energy. This is where we receive great sources of energy, information, and downloads. We have been taught that the sun is bad for our eyes, however, this is not true. A few minutes daily, at sunrise or sunset, is very beneficial. If you find it difficult in the beginning, keep your eyes closed and let your closed eyes and forehead receive the energy, until you get used to it.

I AM Mirror Technique

Your Eyes are the Windows to your Soul. Looking into your eyes, in the mirror, while saying *I AM Affirmations* is an essential Self-Love Discipline. By looking into your eyes, you are connecting with your Soul/Higher Self and strengthening that part of you. You are replacing low-vibrational beliefs about yourself with high-vibrational Truths.

Say these daily to yourself in front of a mirror. (We recommend you say them in front of the mirror for a least 30 days for the fastest Transformation and Healing possible.) You can say them once or multiple times, whatever you feel to do. Look at and feel your heart as you look yourself in the eyes, not only reading the words, but feeling them, as you speak to yourself with Full-Heart Intention.

It may be emotional to say these things to yourself because we are programmed from birth to not fully Love ourselves. As you get comfortable, though, with the I AM Affirmations, after the first 30 days of saying them in front of your mirror, and if you feel guided to do so, also say them while you are doing other activities. Just follow your guidance.

I AM Affirmations:

I AM Nurturing
I AM Childlike Wonder
I AM Laughter
I AM Joy
I AM Grace
I AM Truth
I AM Perseverance
I AM Consistent
I AM Courageous
I AM Wisdom

I AM Divine Intelligence
I AM Inner Strength
I AM Divine Perception
I AM Integrity
I AM Honor
I AM Empathy
I AM Full Feeling
I AM Self-Love
I AM Humble
I AM Accountable
I AM Grateful
I AM Proactive
I AM Genuine
I AM Heart-Centered
I AM Safe
I AM Strong
I AM Powerful
I AM Creative
I AM Worthy
I AM Love
I AM Expressive
I AM Kind
I AM Confident
I AM Abundant

I AM Compassion
I AM Organic
I AM Patient
I AM Tolerant
I AM Responsive
I AM Responsible
I AM Disciplined
I AM Surrender
I AM Passion
I AM Peace
I AM Trust

Conscious or Automatic Writing

Sometimes, our brains can feel like a washing machine with thousands of thoughts going on, creating a feeling of overwhelm as we attach even more thoughts and make stories in our heads. By writing things down and 'emptying your head', those thousands of thoughts actually end up being only a dozen or so. And when you write them down, those dozen thoughts are generally connected to just 2 or 3 real issues or things you need to take action on.

We are all just conduits for Love, and when we empty our vessels and write down our feelings, we make room for Higher Source Energy to come in. There we find Inspiration, Release and Freedom. Stuckness in the body is just trapped emotions, and when you write things down, you are releasing and moving the energy of those emotions. So, use this method as a Spiritual Discipline and see what a difference it makes.

Automatic Writing is when you ask your Higher Self for a message, and you Channel the information exactly as you are receiving it. You begin by saying, *"Thank you, Higher Self, I am ready for our channeling today"* and then you write whatever first comes into your heart/brain. It may be challenging when you begin, however the more you do it, the clearer the messages will become. Doing this with your Higher Self speeds up the Embodiment Process, as you are creating a direct channel for your Higher Self to express through your physical body.

You can also write down and make a list of 5 or more things you are Grateful for each day to help attract more Abundance and Blessings into your life. You can only receive more and grander things and experiences if you are Grateful for what you already have.

Use writing as a tool whenever you need guidance. You can ask your Higher Self/Angels specific questions that you are looking for answers to in the present moment. You can consciously write to get your thoughts out, so they don't stay trapped in your head. You can use Automatic Writing to Channel your Higher Self whenever it is needed. It is a great tool to use to Trust Your Intuition and the Messages You are Receiving.

Oil Pulling (with Coconut Oil)

Your teeth are connected to every organ in your body and, over time, toxins collect in your mouth, which can lead to issues with your teeth, such as cavities or plaque, plus other health issues in the body, in the organ(s) connected to each tooth. When you oil pull first thing in the morning, you extract all those toxins out of your mouth. By adding Turmeric (optional), you also help release density from your pineal gland (third eye).

How to do this:

Add a little Turmeric (optional) to a large tablespoon of Coconut oil (fractionated or unfractionated) and swish it around your mouth for 15-

20 minutes, pushing and pulling it between all your teeth. It is recommended you do this first thing in the morning, before eating or having coffee. (Please don't swallow, spit it in the trashcan, as to not block drains, and then brush your teeth as you normally do.)

Drink Water

Our Light Bodies are upgrading from Carbon DNA to Crystalline DNA (Liquid Crystal). So, it is important to make sure you are drinking a lot of water to assist your body through this process. Water assists in hydrating and lubricating the nervous system (where we process most of our energy). In addition, it moves toxins and density out of the body.

Once you get used to drinking more water, or at least drinking it more consistently, higher water intake will become a more habitual lifestyle. You can Bless Your Water with any higher energy by placing your hand over it and stating what you would like your water to be filled with. For example: *"Thank you for blessing this water with Love, Full Healing, and Positivity".* You can also bless the water with energies for Healing whenever it is necessary or when you feel guided to do so.

Find your Childlike Wonder and Joy

Childlike Wonder is our true essence, a true Present Moment Gift – to be in wonder of the beauty and experience of all things. *What did you Love doing as a child, what did you Love creating, was it painting or building things? Did you Love singing to your favorite music, dancing, or spending time connecting with animals?*

Tap into these things, bring more of that playful side into your life and do more of the things that bring you Joy. When you do that, you Raise Your Vibration, and all the Abundance that is waiting for you will be drawn to you. Everything is Energy! And Joy is one of the highest vibrations you can experience!

During the first 30 days you're working with the Self-Love Disciplines, take time out of each day to Love yourself and do something that brings you True, Soul-Level Joy. If you haven't found something like that yet, take these 30 days to experiment with different creative outlets and see what you like! You can also just do things you find fun!

Although Joy is something you should experience every day (and not just for the first 30 days of the Self-Love Disciplines), once you make the time for yourself to get creative, you will continue to do it as a healthy habit for your everyday life.

Moon and Star Gazing

Just like Sun Gazing, Moon and Star Gazing assists with Connecting to Source Energy. The Codes of Creation are contained in Sacred Geometry, and as the planets move, they create Sacred Geometric Shapes. Shapes create frequencies and sounds, which communicate with our cells and bring Healing. Just stare at the moon and stars (or meditate on them). Pay attention to the messages that come to you.

Conscious Breathing

Take a deep breath in through your nose and fill your belly, hold it for 3 seconds and then breathe out through your mouth. 3 Deep Conscious Breaths will release a lot of tension and relax you. Do this at least once a day.

If there are moments where you are feeling anxious or confused, sit somewhere, and relax. Then take deep breaths in through your nose and out through your mouth until you feel calmer and more centered once again in your inner core.

Move Energy

Energy is meant to be moved, so move your energy!

Any time you are feeling stuck, just move your body – stretch, do some Yoga, create art, clean your space or house, go for a run or walk. Do what makes your body feel good and brings you Joy! Moving energy clears the stagnant energy in your body so that new energy and ideas can flow in.

Utilize Moving Energy as a tool beyond the first 30 days whenever you feel built-up energy in your body. It will allow fresh energy to come in, so you feel clearer and less bogged down by old energies.

Grounding

Grounding is just putting your bare feet on the ground! It sounds simple … because it is! You are connecting your whole body and essence with Mother Earth.

When you Ground, it is like taking handfuls of antioxidants into your body, through your feet. It supports organ function on a cellular level as well. The benefits are huge – Grounding alkalizes your body, reduces inflammation (the cause of all diseases) and allows Healing to naturally occur. 10 minutes a day will make such a difference in your energy, stress levels, sleep and health.

Once you are disciplined in utilizing Grounding, it is an amazing tool to use when you are stressed and need to release energy back into the Earth. The more consistently you use it as a tool, it will become easier to notice when you are ungrounded and need to step outside.

Grounding will always help bring you back to the Present Moment of Now.

Tree Meditation

Trees are alive and carry ancient wisdom, and they are deeply connected to the Earth.

Daily, take a moment to sit by a tree and just stare at it, connect, and pay it attention. Show it Gratitude for the oxygen it gives you to breathe. Take Conscious Breaths and Send It Love. It will communicate with you.

Nature is full of Sacred Geometry, which holds the Codes of Creation. By paying attention to it, nature communicates with you on a cellular level and is incredibly Healing. When you are feeling anxious or stressed, hug a tree, allow it to absorb all the stress from you. Mother Earth knows how to take care of all that for you … just let it go.

Once you are disciplined with your Tree Meditations, you can use a tree whenever you feel you need extra support processing energy. Hugging or Meditating By a Tree is similar to Grounding, but it is a bit more powerful. Utilize the Power of Trees and Mother Earth whenever you feel guided to.

Have a Cold Shower

This resets your energy field and shocks the EGO-Programmed Mind, which leads to Transformation, Healing and Growth.

How so? Because the EGO likes to be comfortable (in a warm shower)! Taking a cold shower is the epitome of discomfort for the EGO, but our True Divine Self doesn’t know discomfort. Only the EGO doesn't like to be uncomfortable. Our Higher Self wants to grow in every way possible, and it's always up for a challenge, no matter how big or small that challenge seems to be to us in our 3D perception.

The water does not have to be ice cold (unless you want it to be). You can jump in a cold or semi-cold shower for as long as you can handle it, whenever you feel guided to do so. You can also turn the water to 'cold' for the last few minutes of your regular shower before you get out. Start with just a few minutes in the cold shower and keep working your way up as your body starts to adjust to the lower temperature.

Use cold showers as a tool whenever you are feeling tired or experiencing low energy as a way to wake up and get more energized.

Cut Energetic Cords

After engaging with people in any shape or form, it is suggested to Cut Cords with them, so their energy is not lingering in your Auric Field. It is especially important to utilize this tool after having any negative or fearful conversations or interactions. You can also do this before you go to sleep each night to clear your energy.

Suggested wording you can use is as follows:

"I cut all energetic cords with everyone and everything I came into contact with today. I re-attach all my energetic cords to everything that is Love, 5D, Heaven on Earth, Source Energy, Whole Truth, and for my Highest Good. I command all atoms and energy that are not mine to go back to the sender, and I command all my atoms and energy back to me in full alignment. And so it is."

"I cut cords with everyone, and everything, and all events. I re-attach all of my energetic cords to everything that is whole, pure, true, and in resonance with Love, magical moments, synchronistic events and Source energy. Thank you, Angels!"

This is a tool you can use daily that, if you stay consistent with it, will become a natural part of your lifestyle. For example, after you hang out with other people, you will naturally Cut Cords when you get home.

The Rainbow Bubble

Energetic Protection is so important in these moments we're now living in. We are each born with a Rainbow Bubble of protective energy around us, but because this is never taught to us or made aware of, we don't use it, and so it weakens. However, we can re-activate it with our Words and Intentions.

Use this as a form of protection whenever you feel you need it. We recommend activating it every time you leave the house by using the following words:

"THANK YOU, ANGELS, FOR THE PROTECTION FROM ALL LOWER ENERGIES BY MY RAINBOW BUBBLE. I AM FULLY PROTECTED. AND SO IT IS." (Then imagine a Rainbow Bubble being placed around you ... and your home/car/workplace/etc.)

You can also activate this bubble of protection around those you Love and care about. Just ask for the Rainbow Bubble to be activated for them.

Use the Violet Flame & Bless Your Food

When we understand that EVERYTHING IS ENERGY, we become Alchemists. The Violet Flame is a powerful transformational tool used by all Alchemists. It can be used in Blessing the Food and Drinks we consume. Hover your hand over your food or drink and pray, using the Violet Flame. Once you start Blessing Your Food consistently, it will become a healthy lifestyle habit that you do naturally.

Examples of the wording you can use (saying it to yourself or out loud):

"Violet Flame, I ask you to transform and bless this meal, transforming all energy in it that is not Love back into Love. May this meal nourish my body, heal it, and bring me joy. And so it is. Thank you."

"Violet Flame, I ask you to go before me, removing all obstacles and highlighting my highest path with magical moments and synchronistic events. And so it is."

Rainbow Sword Technique

The Rainbow Sword Technique is great to utilize any time when you are struggling with lower thoughts or thought loops. Whenever you are experiencing lower thought loops, such as anxiety, worry, or stress, visualize the Rainbow Sword cutting through all those thoughts.

You can also state out loud, *"I cut cords with all thoughts with my Rainbow Sword."*

The more we utilize the Rainbow Sword, the quicker we can transform out of lower thoughts and into higher thoughts.

Rest Consciously

Before you go to sleep, Cut Cords with everyone and everything and then Reattach Them with Love, like you do in the Cutting Energy Cords Practice. Then, Intend and Ask the Angels to assist you in Sleeping Consciously. Also, Ask the Angels to help your body be Protected, Healed, and Rested while you sleep, also asking that you are taken to the Highest Timeline to be of the greatest service to all of Humanity.

It is of great value before you fall asleep to also set your energetic for the next day. For example, you can say something like, *"I will wake up energized, full of joy and excited for the day. Thank you, Angels."*

7 Day Garlic Pineal Cleanse

Garlic is great for the immune system, and it is a powerful, natural antibiotic. In addition, it's also very effective to cleanse the Pineal Gland (the Third Eye). Do this cleanse whenever you feel guided to or feel your body needs a detox:

- Take 1 raw clove of garlic for 7 days
  (*You can go up to 7 cloves per day.*)

  Each day, cut up 1 to 7 cloves of garlic, leave it sit for 15 minutes to oxidize, and then put it on a food or meal of your choice.

  (*A sandwich with egg and mayonnaise seems to be the most palatable as the mayonnaise reduces the burn.*)

This Cleanse takes you on quite an intense detox journey, but it is so worth it!

Ego Death Ceremony

An Ego Death Ceremony can be done one time, daily, weekly, or anytime you feel you want to utilize it. Follow your guidance on what you feel is best for you. This ceremony is very powerful, as its full intention is to dissolve and release the EGO-Programmings.

What is more important than the actual ceremony itself is your Intention with it. Your Intention is powerful, which is why we suggest you follow your guidance in terms of how many times you feel you need to do it.

To perform the Ego Death Ceremony, simply write down on a piece of paper, *"I dissolve the following Programmings and release the following Ego frequencies ..."*

Next, include any and all EGO-Programmings you want to release, using as many as you would like. Then burn the paper!

On the next few pages, you'll find a listing of the Ego Traits. Choose the ones that you feel you have and write them down.

Ego Traits:

LACK OF WISDOM

LACK OF EXPERIENCE

LACK OF COMPASSION

LACK OF PASSION

LACK OF PERCEPTION

LACK OF INTEGRITY

LACK OF HONOR

LACK OF EMPATHY

LACK OF FEELING

LACK OF SELF-LOVE

UNWORTHINESS

CHILDHOOD TRAUMA

CHILDISH BEHAVIOR

ROBOTIC HABITS

HATRED OF MASCULINE OR FEMININE

PREFERENCE TO PAIN & SUFFERING

SUPERIORITY

THINKING YOU KNOW BETTER

ENTITLEMENT

SELF-IMPORTANCE

DELUSIONS OF GRANDEUR

FANTASY

NEEDING TO BE RIGHT

CONTROLLING

UNGRATEFUL

NO ACCOUNTABILITY

SPREADING OR PARTICIPATION IN GOSSIP/JEALOUSY

VANITY

LACK OF BEAUTY

DESIRE (OR WANTING TO BE DESIRED)

VALIDATION

WANTING TO FOLLOW OR BE FOLLOWED

FAKE
(UNABLE TO BE GENUINE OR COMPULSIVE LYING)

REVERENCE OF THE MIND

SEEKING REVERENCE

REVERENCE OF ANIMALS

JUSTIFICATION

PROCRASTINATION

BARGAINING

POVERTY CONSCIOUSNESS
(ALWAYS THINKING IN THE ENERGY OF LACK)

ADDICTION TO SUGAR

LINEAR THINKING AND ACTING

IGNORANCE
(AND IGNORING LOVE)

ARROGANCE

ATTACHMENT
(TO PEOPLE, PLACES AND THINGS)

TAKING
(FROM HUMANITY & THE PLANET)

INCUBUS & SUCCUBUS ENERGY
(THE TAKING OF ENERGY THROUGH WORDS, TOUCH, SEX AND OTHER ABILITIES)

PRINCE/PRINCESS CONDITIONING

BITCH CONDITIONING

ASSHOLE CONDITIONING

ANAL-RETENTIVE

SEVERE IMPATIENCE

EASILY DISTRACTED

QUITTER

INCONSISTENT

COMPLAINING

LAZINESS

COMPLACENT

REACTIVE

CULTURAL PROGRAMMING
(I.E., WHITE PROGRAMMING, WHITE TRASH PROGRAMMING, ETC.)

BLOODLUST
(WANTING TO SEE OR THE AROUSAL FROM SEEING BLOODSHED)

SUPER EGO
(AN ADVANCED FORM OF EGO CHARACTERIZED BY EXTREME ARROGANCE, THINKING YOU KNOW BETTER, FANTASY, OR RACING THOUGHT LOOPS)

SPIRITUAL EGO
(THE FANTASY VERSION OF SPIRITUALITY, WHERE ONE THINKS THEY HAVE ATTAINED ENLIGHTENMENT WHEN THEY HAVEN'T AND THINKS THEY ARE

ABOVE OTHERS AND THEREFORE, LACK ACCOUNTABILITY)

Higher-Self Ceremony

Utilize this Higher-Self Ceremony to assist with greater Higher-Self Embodiment, as well as to increase the Divine Energy flowing through you. Choose as many Divine Traits as you feel called to work with (or all of them) and do a ceremony. You can break up the Divine Traits and do weekly ceremonies as well. Follow your guidance and choose what works best for you. Just remember that your Intention is more important than the number of ceremonies you do.

Start by writing this:

"Dear All of Creation, I am so thankful for all your Loving Support and Guidance. I am so Grateful that I embody fully and completely the following traits in the Present Moment of Now..."

The next few pages that follow have the list of the Divine Traits that you can add to your ceremony.

Divine Traits:

Wisdom
Experience
Compassion

Passion
Perception
Integrity
Honor
Full Feeling
Unconditional Self-Love
Worthiness
Acceptance
Embracement
Surrender
Allowance
Humility
Non-Attachment
Giving
Receiving
Childlike Wonder
Preference for Love
"I don't know shit!"
Secure
Trust
Beauty
Balanced Harmonics
Empowerment
Power (with a real appreciation of the heart)

Respect of the Heart
Appreciation of and Respect for Animals
Appreciation of and Respect for Nature
Full Accountability
Proactivity
Divine Will
Full Gratitude
Embracement of Grandness
Present Moment of Now
Surrender to Harmony
Grace
Flow
Gratitude for Food
Multi-Dimensional Perspective
Internalization
Goddess and God Consciousness
Self-Worth
Self-Respect
Full Focus
Patience
Consistency
Pure Presence
Non-Resistant Body Flow
Heaven on Earth Within

Fearless
Diamond Heart
Unified Field of Love
Limitlessness
Authentic Higher-Self
Joy and Fulfillment
My Highest Path and Timeline
Freedom
The Universal Laws
The Divine Decrees
Unity
Innocence
Truth
Peace

End your ceremony by writing:

"Thank you, Angels, that I am a Lover, Giver, and of the Highest Light, emanating Bliss and experiencing Heaven. I am Eternal, Present in the Moment of Now, and full of Gratitude. I am committed to being disciplined and in service to Love and Humanity. Thank you, and so it is."

Other Ceremonies

Ceremonies are powerful tools for Transformation, Release, Embodiment, and Intention Setting. You can do simple ceremonies whenever you are guided to and/or during powerful energetic days (such as new and full moons).

We are all in physical vessels here on Planet Earth, however, we are also anchoring in 5D-Consciousness into our physicality. This requires both energetic and physical work. Ceremonies are the perfect tool with which to integrate the process. This is true Manifestation.

Ceremonies are best done for the following purposes:

- -transforming lower energetics
- -releasing grief or trauma
- -anchoring in our Higher-Self
- -setting Intentions for Manifestations

When we do ceremonies, it is great to bring in the power of the different elements of nature, including earth, water, fire, and crystals. Use your Intuition and Guidance on whether to bury your ceremony, burn it, place it in a body of water, or charge it with a crystal. (Burying a ceremony is best used when planting Intentions. Burning a ceremony is best used for Transforming and Embodying. Placing your ceremony in a body of water is best for Releasing, Cleansing and Healing. Crystals are best used to energize your ceremony when you are sending Intentions out to the planet.)

It is always best to begin by setting your Intention for the ceremony. *Is this a ceremony for your own Release, Healing, Embodiment, Transformation and Manifestation? Or, is this a ceremony of Intention for Humanity or the planet?*

Once you have your Intention set, then feel into what elements you would like to use in your ceremony. This is an organic process. There are no wrong ways to do a ceremony!

We recommend beginning your ceremony with Gratitude to Source, your Angels, the Galactics, and/or your Higher Self, setting the tone of Gratefulness for what you're Intending.

Final Notes

Letting Go Of Ego-Programming takes Time, Patience and Consistency. The Disciplines and Tools outlined in this book will serve your Highest Purpose and allow you to embody your Higher Self the fastest way possible.

Be gentle with yourself while you are Healing; do not beat yourself up if things do not go as planned or as intended. Take Accountability, Trust everything happens for a reason, and Let It Go. Every experience is helping you grow on a soul-level.

When you feel yourself becoming overwhelmed, come back to the Present Moment. Breathe and be Grateful for the Present Moment of Now. When you are Grateful for the small things, you will be given more to be Grateful for. Then, you Create Space for Miracles to happen … because you've learned how to let go of worry and fear-based thoughts.

You got this!

CHAPTER TWENTY-FOUR: ASCENSION 101 TRAINING PROGRAM

COURSE 1: WHAT IS ASCENSION?

The Ascension (or Awakening) is a 'remembering' more than a 'learning' or 'seeking'. Our cosmic origin is embedded within our DNA and, once our physical vessel is ready to handle the Process of Awakening, it activates.

Awakening begins differently for each soul, but many find that when they have reached rock bottom, a place of pain, suffering, depression, fear, or despair ... the Light turns on. Or when our belief systems or "life as we know it" are suddenly shattered by a revelation, a piece of information, a relationship, or a calling, our Awakening begins.

Once this point of shifting starts, it can never be stopped. In other words, *once you begin seeing through the Veil of Illusion, you can never go back.*

For many souls, this is why their Awakening takes so long. Every soul on the planet (except those of the Dark, who are considered to be aberrations) has a Higher Self that is navigating their human vessel/personality through their current lifetime. The Higher Self cannot come through to the vessel, however, if the vessel is traumatized, wounded, in the EGO Mind, or is low vibrational. For this reason, many souls never wake up – the shock to their consciousness through an Awakening would be too overwhelming for them to handle (physically, mentally, and emotionally).

Once the soul has passed a certain amount of Life Lessons, and it reaches a point of desperation within the human experience, this is when there is enough Heart Opening to allow the Higher Self to come through. The Higher Self then orchestrates many tests, challenges, and choice points for the Human Self to experience, in order to prepare the vessel for the Anchoring In of the Higher Self.

Awakening is the process of Undoing, Remembering, and De-Programming. It is the return to Childlike Wonder, Unconditional Love, Freedom, Truth, and Reunion with Source. This process can be painful, but it is also beautiful and incredibly profound. It is the only real thing in existence … The Soul's Journey Home to Source.

This process will require Physical Healing, Emotional Healing, Mental Healing and Spiritual Healing. It also requires Self-Love, Dedication, Surrender, and Trust. Many belief systems and attachments are purged in the alchemical fires of the Ascension Process, and this is where we often experience it as painful. However, this process is truly about ripping the bandages off the wounds that already have come loose by giving them Attention and Healing. This is how we transcend pain and suffering.

HOMEWORK

Read through the *Insights* below, which is a list of very simple, but profound Truths that form the basis of Awakening. Become familiar with the terms and concepts, as they will become a core part of your journey and experience.

Begin your journey through this course by Journaling. Be consistent with this as it will become one of your greatest tools. Document your thoughts, your feelings, your ideas, and your experiences. This helps you process the energy you will be sensing and feeling.

Lastly, Focus on Your Breath. Spend at least a few minutes each day focusing on breathing in deep breaths through your nose, and then exhaling slowly through your mouth. Cut out all thoughts and focus only on the feeling and process of breathing. While doing this, we recommend visualizing Breathing in Love and Breathing out Love, which raises the Vibration of your environment.

INSIGHTS

- ❖ All Energy must be expressed either Consciously or unconsciously. If your environment, experiences, or life do not reflect Joy, Abundance, Growth, and Love, then you are unconsciously (versus Consciously) creating your reality.

- ❖ All pain, illness or disease is based on energetics. Every ailment within the body has an energetic root cause and an emotional root cause. You can Heal any ailment if you Heal the underlying energetic.

- ❖ Any thought that does not bring you Joy or Inspiration is based in EGO/lower thought.

- ❖ What you resist persists; what you look at, you Let Go Of.

- Accept, Embrace, and Allow.

- Triggers are treasures. Anything you do not like in another, exists in you.

- If something is not working for you, Change it. If something is working for you, do not Change it. Doing the same thing over and over, and expecting a different result, is insanity.

- We are all God with God.

- Source is Feminine, the Yin, the Inner (Internal). She exists within us all; she birthed our souls. The Masculine is the Outer (External), the Yang, the structure and direction of feminine energy.

- Awareness transforms into Consciousness.

- Love and the Unknown are the only real energies in existence.

- Non-Attachment is true Freedom.

- Be the Change you wish to see.

- The Present Moment of Now is where all things exist.

- Separation is an illusion.

- What is Real will always remain.

- Nothing in existence can be known, only Felt.

- *We don't know shit!*

- There are no mistakes. Everything is either a Lesson or a Blessing.

- Surrender is the key.

- ❖ Do not lead with words, Lead with Action. Lead by Example.

- ❖ Trust the process.

- ❖ When in doubt, Ask your Angels for 3 Synchronicities (Confirmations/Confirms).

- ❖ Do not take ANYTHING personally. Only the EGO gets offended.

COURSE 2: RE-HEART THE STORY OF CREATION

Earth is the only planet still existing in 3D-Consciousness. It's the lowest vibrational planet in existence. Earth was a school for souls to incarnate into physical bodies to experience the illusion of separation and duality in order to then obtain greater Wisdom and Experience.

The Dark Ones overtook Earth over 27,000 years ago, after the fall of Atlantis and Lemuria. Lemuria was in 5D-Consciousness, and Atlantis was in 3D/4D Vibrations. Both were inhabiting Earth at the same time. Mother of All Creation was Queen of Lemuria, and many of the incarnated 144,000 remember their lifetime in Lemuria. Mother

God was betrayed by her husband Horus, who gave the Atlanteans 5D Technology, which they could not use while being in 3D Frequencies.

When the Atlanteans used the 5D Technology, it caused an explosion between the timelines. Mother God had to quickly make the choice to ascend (which is much different than Ascension from the 3rd Dimension) to stop the planet/Humanity from going into a blackhole. This set back the planet fully into 3D. Many Lemurians died during the explosion, but some escaped to Inner Earth; others were taken captive by the Atlanteans.

With Mother God off the planet, the Anunnaki came down and pretended to be gods. They took the Dream Machine Technology and implanted the first fearful thought into the Collective Consciousness – that we are separate from God. This planted more fearful thoughts into Humanity, where they forgot their God Selves/Mother and Father God. After that, the Anunnaki created the EGO-Programmed Mind, as a way to keep Humanity in states of fear and low consciousness, so they could continue to inhabit Earth and have control over it, being as they could not exist in the higher frequencies of Love.

Despite the efforts of the Dark, Earth began her Ascension Process and began moving back into the Light. As Humanity struggled to get out of the EGO Mind, their souls came to Mother of All Creation, begging her to assist them. Mother and Father God agreed and began physically incarnating on Earth with the 144,000.

This Programming is so deep that no one has been able to make it out of the illusion … until now. Mother and Father God, as well as the 144,000 original souls, have been incarnating on Earth for thousands of years, attempting to ascend the planet. But they were killed every time before they were able to do so.

Finally, however, Mother did it. She made it out of the Matrix and has transformed all the pain and suffering for Humanity. She had a 1 in 7.8 billion chance of making it, and she busted all the odds. This moment has been prophesied many times, and now it is here.

Every soul that is incarnated on the planet at this time has agreed to participate in the Ascension Process. Earth is going back to 5D Frequencies, and it means everyone must do the same, whether or not they are Consciously aware of this Truth at this time. Everybody has a unique role in this Ascension, as everyone has a unique role to play in All of Creation.

Once the Anunnaki knew they could not win against the Light and the inevitable Ascension Process, they surrendered back home into the Light. Then, the Illuminati took over. They had a group of beings who were their slaves, known as the Cabal. Once the Illuminati realized they also could not win against the Light, they also surrendered and went back to the Light.

The Illuminati begged the Cabal to surrender; however, they refused. The Cabal came into full power in 1996, after the Illuminati surrendered. Since then, the Cabal have been in control of the planet, up until recently, when they lost power to the White Hats/Mother and Father God/The Galactic Federation of Light. The Ascension is now inevitable, as all Darkness has no power on the planet anymore now that Mother God/Mother Earth fully completed her Ascension Process.

The Anunnaki and Atlanteans split the right brain and left brain, causing distortions, imbalance, and illusion. The Ego-Programmed Mind was placed into the left brain, so that they could control Humanity. Through the disconnection that occurred, Humanity forgot who they were (which is done by the right brain/God-Consciousness), so it was then easy for the Anunnaki and Atlanteans to enslave Humanity. With all the illusory belief systems, rules, and fear they installed, it was easy to continue to manipulate the Collective. Then, they trained Humanity to serve the Darkness, to become their servants of the Darkness using illusionary fears that were never real.

The right side of the brain is the Creative, Multi-Dimensional God Self, the Higher Connection to the Etheric Realm, Higher Thoughts and God Consciousness. It is your Connection to 5D, Mother God, the Galactic's, and your Higher Self. Higher Thoughts are unlimited, they're shared within the Collective Consciousness, and All Possibilities exist in 5D and beyond.

The left side of the brain is the intellectual/logical aspect. When out of sync with the right, it connects into the primitive reptilian mind (and to the illusion of outside attachments). All outside attachments are thus an illusion.

Now, however, the brain is returning to its Original Form, meaning the right and left brain are being "Fused Together" to Create Complete Awakening into Full Consciousness. This fusion that is taking place is an Unstoppable Event, FOR ALL HUMAN BEINGS ON PLANET EARTH TO GET BACK TO FULL GOD CONSCIOUSNESS.

Our advice is to Allow, Embrace, and Let Go Of all belief systems, all illusions, and EVERYTHING Humanity has ever been taught or told. Currently, those who are resisting are only hiding their Light behind Fear.

HOMEWORK

Feel into the information that has been shared. Feel into anything that it triggers, or anything that gives your body *'light ups'* or chills. Trust what resonates with you.

Try the following brain activation before you rest (and use it as many times as you'd like to):

"Thank you, Higher Self, Angels, Galactics, and Source for all Divine Downloads, Upgrades, and Codes. I Embrace, Accept and Allow All Healing. I ask for all Brain Upgrades, DNA Activations, and Heart Healing.

I command my right brain to overtake my left brain, and for my brain to merge back into oneness. I command my brain to activate its full usage and full consciousness."

Next, visualize your brain being lit up with Rainbow/Plasma Light. Allow it to Heal Your Brain, Activate Your Pineal Gland, and Connect All Neural Pathways. Allow the Rainbow Light to clear out any and all brain density, toxins, heavy metals, and both physical and etheric implants.

COURSE 3: MISSION EARTH ACTIVATED

Once Planet Earth was knocked down in Consciousness, and the Atlantean Experiments began, Mother and Father of Creation, along with the 144,000 and many other brave souls from around the cosmos, began incarnating. We knew the only way to ascend the planet was from the inside out.

All of you reading this have lived many lifetimes before. If you feel that your soul is relatively new, you may have had less lifetimes than others, but nonetheless, you are the most equipped to be here on the planet NOW.

Once the Dark Ones realized that all the Angels were incarnating here, they opened up portals to bring in ALL lower entities and lower beings. This is why Earth is the final battleground. What the Dark did not anticipate was that, once all lower entities and beings came into this realm, the portals would be closed. So, all of the Dark Beings/Entities are currently trapped here on Earth and cannot leave.

The process of Earth's Planetary Ascension, then, is to Raise Our Vibrations, Dissolve the EGO-Programming, and thus Raise the Consciousness of the Planet to a Level the Dark Can No Longer Exist At. This will dissolve them, and they will be recycled by the Galactic Central Sun.

This is the final lifetime and the chosen Ascension Point. It has been prophesied by many civilizations, including the Mayans and Hopis. December 21, 2012 marked the day that the Ascension truly began, as Earth entered the 5th Dimension (5D).

Since then, we have slowly been climbing up the ladder of Ascension, battling through many attempts of the Dark to thwart the plan. We are currently flying through the photon belt at lightning speed, bringing more and more Light onto the planet.

In order to secure the liberation of Earth, the Astral Realm was dissolved in 2009 by Mother of Creation and the Galactics. The Astral was the holding place for the lower entities, who were occupying the 4D Realm, manipulating energies from that realm.

We can now see 4D as a void space; it is essentially a place of time and space that exists between 3D and 5D, which is where we are currently residing as a Collective. The 3D Realm is collapsing, and so we are in the void of the Unknown (4D) as we go through the first ever Physical Planetary Ascension. All who are un-awakened are still clinging to the 3D Plane. Just the Astral portion of 4D was dissolved, so 4D still exists, but it is a void space, and it's typically where those reside who are going through massive Transformation and the Unknown, until they can anchor fully into the 5D Frequency, which means we have dissolved our EGO and established ourselves fully into the 5D Plane. First-wavers must anchor into 5D first in order to stabilize the rest of Planet Earth while it's moving through the 3D-4D transition.

HOMEWORK

Do this exercise when you are in a centered place. Cut Cords with all lower thoughts, all fears, and all external events. Sit in a Meditative Position (whatever you are comfortable with) with a Journal.

Take 3 Deep Breaths, in through the nose and out through the mouth. Ask your Higher Self to share any information with you, including any guidance, information, or images.

Sit with yourself and don't try and force anything. Just Allow Things to Flow Through to You. Most importantly, do NOT doubt anything that is coming through.

Start Writing Down anything that is coming to you. Keep writing until you feel like you have gotten through all that is coming forth. If you are struggling to receive anything, then practice just Sitting Still, Breathing, and Feeling Into Your Body. This will help increase your ability to Feel and Strengthen Your Feeling Centers.

Document in your journal how you feel and any sensations you notice.

COURSE 4: AGE OF AQUARIUS CODES

The Golden Age of Aquarius (5D), which the planet entered in 2012, is vastly different from the Kali Yuga or Dark Age of Pisces that we have been in for the last 27,000 years. During the Age of Pisces, it was all about creating illusions, essentially magic tricks, to keep Humanity in the Darkness.

With this Age, we saw the lower energies of Pisces unfold – illusion, fantasy, hierarchies, victim consciousness, and addictions. The Age of Aquarius is a much different energy.

The Age of Aquarius is all about the Freedom of Information. No longer can secrets and lies be hidden in the Dark. No longer can Truths be kept from Humanity. Aquarius is also about Community and the gathering with others for a Higher Purpose. In Pisces, we were so focused on survival, we could not truly give to or help others. We fell into deep self-importance.

In order to be a match to 5D, we must accept the Aquarian Codes of Community, Unity-Consciousness, Service to the Greater Good, and Acceptance and Tolerance of ALL. Only Lovers and Givers will inherit Planet Earth; all those who are stuck in low frequencies, the Takers, will be removed.

This is the Age of Awakening. Truth will Set Us All Free.

The first step in embracing the Aquarian Codes is to be Open to All New Information. The way we have functioned on this planet is to reject information that threatens a belief system we have. We only seek information that reinforces our current belief systems, which keeps us trapped in illusion.

So … forget everything you think you know. Empty out all your belief systems. This is when cosmic knowledge can then come to you. This is when your Higher Self can connect with you. Actively observe yourself and how your belief systems control your thoughts, actions, and behaviors.

Be Conscious of where you hold judgments of yourself and others. Judgment was the Age of Pisces, based on the false belief that God was judgmental and served punishment and wrath. The Truth is that God is not capable of such energy, only Humanity is. Our judgments are based on belief systems of right and wrong, good and bad, all of which must be dissolved. All is simply Experience.

Once you have begun dissolving these false beliefs, you will able to process more and more of the Intuitive Guidance of Truth.

HOMEWORK

Take a piece of paper and write down all belief systems you currently have. This will include anything that you categorize as "good", "bad", "right" or "wrong". If you cannot feel into what your belief systems are, here are some examples:

- -the belief that one needs to be "pure" or "good" in order be a part of God
- -the belief that one must work "hard" in order to succeed in life
- -the belief that certain foods are "bad" for you
- -the belief that things like alcohol or tobacco are "bad" for you
- -the belief that things must make logical sense in order to be true
- -the belief that certain things should be done at certain times
- -the belief that people “never change”
- -the belief that when you get older, you will get sick and die
- -the belief that anything outside of yourself can bring you joy or sadness

Take time to feel into each of these belief systems and where they come from. Most likely, they will have come from your parents or family. Then, Cut Cords with these belief systems and see how you feel.

COURSE 5: EVERYTHING IS ENERGY

EVERYTHING IN EXISTENCE IS ENERGY.

Every single atom of Consciousness carries an Energetic Vibrational Frequency. In this 3D Realm, we are limited to our five senses (touch, taste, smell, sight, and sound). But this is less than 1% of ALL energy in existence. When we operate ONLY based on what we can sense (with our five senses), we are cutting out 99% of the energy that is communicating with us.

Every action we take, every word we speak, and every single thing we have Manifested in our Earthly experiences was a product of OUR energy. This is what many living in the mind fail to comprehend. The mind can only interpret information it understands (through the five senses); it cannot understand anything outside of that.

For instance, if you keep attracting similar experiences into your life, such as dysfunctional relationships, lack of abundance, or lack of support, this is a mirror reflection of the energy you are carrying. Once you understand this, it shifts your perspective.

All energy MUST be expressed, either consciously or unconsciously. Most of what we perceive and understand, however, is based on the conscious energy we are expressing. We fail to sense and see our UNCONSCIOUS energy, which is what we call the Shadow Side/Programming/EGO. For example, if you are having a conversation with someone, and the other person has a reaction to something that you are saying, you may think, *that's not what I said* or *that's not what I meant*. Two things are happening here:

1. You are giving off an unconscious energy that goes deeper than the surface level words you are speaking, and this is what the other person is reacting to or misunderstanding.
2. The other person carries the same frequency, which is why it is triggering them, causing a reaction.

Most of our misunderstandings between humans are because we are unaware of the unconscious energy we are putting out, and because our words and actions often do not match our frequency. This causes us to be out of integrity, fake, inconsistent, and unaccountable.

Once you Begin To Notice The Energetic Patterns Within Your Life, you can start to reflect on where the unconscious energy is within you. This will stem from stored trauma/wounding, EGO-Programming, denial, or lack of accountability.

When we START LOOKING AT EVERYTHING AS ENERGY, rather than the surface level story we're expressing, we stop taking things personally. Everything that occurs in our external world is a mirror of us, but also, at the same time, it is not personal. It's simply energy expressing itself. When we are in the mind, though, we cannot see ourselves (or the reflections of ourselves). This is the game of The Illusion. Thus, we unconsciously create a reality that attempts to show us what is within us, by mirroring it back to us.

Most beings do not take accountability for this, and instead, they immediately want to blame, point fingers, and project onto others why their reality is not as they wish it to be. We do this with relationships, jobs, government, media, and more. We BLAME, and we PLAY THE VICTIM.

This journey is entirely internal. Therefore, all Transformation must first occur internally before it can take place externally. This is why the initial stages of Awakening can be quite painful. We must face all that has been stuffed down, bypassed, and neglected within us. We must Take Accountability for the reality we have created.

Although painful, this process is what allows us to Heal. This is what allows us to find our True Selves and to Empower Ourselves as Co-Creators with Source, which Changes Our Reality.

HOMEWORK

Reflect on the energetic patterns in your life, thus far. Feel into any Repeating Patterns that have come up for you. The tests and challenges always give you a clue as to where you are being called to evolve. When we do not pass the tests, they will repeat, often in different ways but with the same energy.

The easiest way to identify a repeating pattern is to feel into the moments when you often think, *"I always ______"* or *"I never_____."*

Examples:

"I always end up being hurt."
"I never have any support."

Reflect on what energies within you are creating these patterns. These will typically be tied to your belief systems on wounding. When we have experienced trauma or wounding in our lives, and they go unhealed, we create experiences over and over to trigger that same wounding.

Write A Ceremony and ask to become aware of all the unconscious energy within you. Ask to Begin Healing any unconscious wounding you have. Feel Into what areas need to be worked on within yourself.

COURSE 6: THE EGO-PROGRAMMED MIND

As previously mentioned, the EGO-Programmed Mind was implanted into the Collective Consciousness by the Atlanteans and the Anunnaki. The root of the EGO is Fear, which is the opposite of Love. The EGO was designed similar to a computer virus, and once it was implanted into the Collective Consciousness, it could root itself so deep into the psyche that, it could pass onto future generations through the DNA.

The Anunnaki did this because of their great fear of Humanity Waking Up, which would Raise the Consciousness to a Vibration they could no longer exist in. They did not want to let go of their control of

Earth. The Cabal minions were then placed in high levels of the Elite, including royal families, politicians, bankers, and large corporations.

The EGO ensured that Humanity would keep themselves enslaved, through Fear. The root of all dysfunctions on the planet is based in EGO Frequencies. For example:

The EGO Frequencies of Dysfunction:

- -War: fear, power over, competition
- -Poverty: lack consciousness, fight or flight
- -Abuse: trauma, wounding, guilt, anger
- -Death: fear
- -Pain & Suffering: fear, attachment, belief systems

The EGO-Programmed Mind functions based on hiding itself. The EGO actually fears Fear itself.

EGO first developed as the "survival instinct". During our primitive history, we lived in a constant state requiring survival instincts – for example, we learned how to create fire to keep warm and cook our food, we figured out how to hunt for food, how to build shelter from the elements, etc.

As we evolved, though, the EGO became more sophisticated, which created deeper levels of pain and suffering. This resulted in warfare, domination, hierarchy, and slavery. We became not only afraid of the outside world, but also afraid of other humans.

We then developed massive amounts of diseases and illnesses, as a product of Fear living in our DNA. We experienced or witnessed poverty, homelessness, and starvation.

Societies continued to evolve and create even more ways to enslave themselves. We created "nations", with borders, government, rules, systems, and additional control mechanisms. Societies and cultures also began passing on these deep-rooted belief systems to keep everyone in separation.

Our current society faces illnesses of poisons, toxins, addictions, distractions, fear, self-importance, and being hooked on information and mental processes.

At the same time, however, we're limited in our ability to accept and process all the new information we have such unprecedented and immediate access to. And when this information challenges our belief systems, we then challenge the information itself. The EGO is a defense mechanism built into the brain to deny anything disrupting what it already knows. Therefore, the EGO can ONLY think based on the past or to worry about the future.

The EGO cannot be in the Present Moment of Now because that is the Unknown. LOVE is the only answer to dissolving the EGO. And it's also how we dissolve the 3D belief systems, lower thoughts, reactions, judgments, and defenses.

This process takes time, as part of the dissolving of the EGO is Healing our trauma and wounding. Trauma and wounding are the main ways that we are kept in Fear Frequencies. All beings hold trauma and wounding, both from this life and previous lives.

The Awakening Process is organic and cannot be rushed. The key is to not take anything personally, to know that you are a Royal Angel, and to Trust in your Connection to Source. The Heart is the portal to New Earth, and where we will find our True Self.

HOMEWORK

Read through the complete list of EGO Frequencies below and feel into how each of these frequencies are shown in the Collective, and within you. Feel into the ones you know are your biggest bits of EGO-Programmings.

Next, do an EGO Death Ceremony. Use the *EGO Death Ceremony Guide* for reference, which you can download from our website at 5DFullDisclosure.org. Write down all the frequencies you know you have. (You can always do all of them, if you feel so guided.) Then … Burn Your List. Do this as often as you feel you need to. These ceremonies are powerful and help speed up your Transformation Process.

Next, read through the Divine Traits again and feel into each one of those. Identify those you feel you have not fully anchored in yet, or that you are struggling to anchor in, and write them down. Next, grab a piece of paper and write down all the traits you would like to anchor in deeper, prefacing them with the phrase *"I AM"*.

For example, if Discipline or Integrity are on your list, you would write:

"I AM Disciplined."
"I AM in Integrity."

Use your list to do *I AM Mirror Affirmations* 1-2x per day.

COURSE 7: TRANSFORMATIONAL TOOLS

As we go through the Process of EGO Dissolvement and Healing, we can always rely on our Transformation Tools and Spiritual Disciplines. Used consistently, they keep us Grounded, Centered, and In Surrender.

Examples include:

- Grounding
  (placing your feet on the Earth for at least 2-5 minutes per day)

- Meditation
  (this can be done in traditional style – for example, seated in lotus pose using various hand mudras – or while doing any task in which you are in the Present Moment of Now, such as Walking Meditation, which is simply meditating while you walk)

- Cold Showers

- Automatic Writing

- Cutting Cords
- Sun Gazing (or Moon and Star Gazing)
- Shielding (for example, using the Rainbow Bubble)
- Using the Rainbow, Violet, Emerald, or Golden Flames for Healing and Transmuting Energy
- Ceremonies
- Prayer
- Mirror Affirmations

The key is to discover what works best for you. Try different tools and techniques and feel free to create your own. You also may switch between different tools and disciplines, depending on what your needs are.

The KEY is CONSISTENCY. The EGO cannot and will not be consistent on its own. The tools and disciplines you use need your consistency in order to have the greatest effects. Many may use their tools on the days they are struggling, but on the days they feel good, will not do them, which can slow your Ascension Process.

The more consistent you are, the more stable your energy will become, so that you will be able to ride the waves of energy without crashing. Do at least ONE Discipline or use at least ONE Tool, EVERYDAY. Then feel free to add in and switch up the other tools and disciplines, based on your guidance.

We suggest Mirror Affirmations, Daily Movement, and Automatic Writing as your Daily Disciplines, adding in others as you go. These three are the most powerful tools for moving energy and anchoring in the Higher-Self.

HOMEWORK

Practice using some of the Tools & Disciplines throughout your day and see how they make you feel. Experiment with different ones and variations of each to find what works for you.

Recommendations for Specific Purposes are as Follows:

For assistance with grounding your energy:

- Movement
- Grounding
- Deep Breathing

For assistance when you are spinning in an energy:

- Cut Cords
- Cold Showers
- Ceremonies

For assistance with opening up your connection to your Higher Self:

- Automatic Writing
- Sun Gazing
- Prayer

For assistance with anchoring in your Higher Self:

- Mirror Affirmations
- the Rainbow Flame
- Meditation

COURSE 8: BALANCED HARMONICS

Now that you are becoming familiar with the EGO Frequencies as well as the Divine Traits, we are ready to focus on Balanced Harmonics. Balanced Harmonics is the balance of our Internal Feminine and Masculine.

Many dysfunctions have developed within the Collective and in masculine/feminine relationships due to internal imbalances. The organic/natural Balanced Harmonics are:

- *-Feminine: 51% Feminine / 49% Masculine*
- *-Masculine: 51% Masculine / 49% feminine*

When we are energetically imbalanced, this causes us to energetically seek out others who are on the opposite end of the spectrum, in order to balance ourselves out. This happens most frequently in relationships, but can also occur in friendships, partnerships, and connections.

For instance, if one is heavily imbalanced in their masculine energy, they have an over-abundance of aggression, logical thinking, and control. One in this state lacks the feminine balance of feeling, compassion, receptivity, and openness. So, they choose someone who is very feminine to partner with. The same would occur in a vice versa situation.

As a Collective, we can see how this has plagued us. The feminine have become hyper-feminine and the masculine have become hyper-masculine. The feminine became disempowered, overly emotional, always seeking validation, and lacking in boundaries. The masculine became controlling, powering over others, aggressive and numb to their feelings and emotions.

Similarly, this can happen when a feminine becomes overly masculine or a masculine becomes overly feminine. This is what creates the energetic imbalance which causes a feminine to seek out another feminine or a masculine to seek out another masculine.

Every person we are "attracted to" is based on our external seeking of a balance to our own energetics.

In Order To Anchor In Balanced Harmonics, We Must Do The Inner Work. This takes Honesty and Transparency within ourselves. We must actively work on Anchoring In the Divine Traits of the energies we are lacking in, transforming the lower energetics we are holding.

This is the key to anchoring in Heaven on Earth, as 5D Only Resonates With Balance And Purity; it will note anchor in amidst dysfunction and imbalance.

HOMEWORK

Read through the Divine Traits once again, and reflect on those you have written down that you feel you're lacking in. Notice if you are lacking more in Divine Masculine Traits or Divine Feminine Traits.

For example:

- -Divine Masculine Traits include Yang Energy – Passion, Discipline, Integrity, Honor, Tenacity, Empowerment, Truth, Perseverance, Courage, and Bravery
- -Divine Feminine Traits include Yin energy – Receptivity, Compassion, Full Feeling, Intuition, Joy, Tolerance, Openness, and Surrender

If you are lacking in Divine Masculine Traits, your job is to work on your own Empowerment. Speaking your Truth, Drawing Boundaries, Taking Action, and Being Disciplined will assist you in anchoring this in.

If you are lacking in Divine Feminine Traits, your job is to FEEL MORE. This often takes time, as we were programmed not to feel, but rather to think. Practice Letting Go, Trusting in the Universe rather than trying to control it, Expressing Yourself Vulnerably, and Holding Compassion for others rather than judgment.

COURSE 9: ANGELS and GUIDES

Every being on the planet (besides the aberrations such as the Cabal), holds a soul that is connected to Source. We are all Angels having a Human Experience. In addition, each being is assigned a team of Angels and Guides to assist them on their journey. Most often, we have a team of Angels and Guides during our life on Earth, and once we awaken and begin rising to greater levels of mastery, a new team is assigned to us.

Many of our Guides are family members and ancestors who have passed over, as they are part of our DNA lineage and are part of the same Soul Pod. Our Angels are specifically assigned to us, based on a match to our energetics.

The number of Angels and Guides varies from person to person, and the number may change throughout one's Human journey. Our Angelic Team is here to guide us, encourage us, and to provide us with information relevant to our journey.

Forming a connection with your Angels and Guides is essential for your journey. One can always connect directly to Source, as well as to their Higher Self, but your team of Angels and Guides have been specifically tasked with assisting you. THEY ARE ALWAYS WAITING TO BE ASKED FOR HELP.

Angels communicate in various ways, and each being will receive guidance in a different way. They often communicate through Synchronistic Numbers or Words, and they also give direct communication, when asked. Opening up to your connection with your Angels requires Trust. When you doubt or choose not to listen to your Intuition, you are shutting down the connection.

Automatic Writing is the best tool for connecting with your Higher Self and your Angels. Writing down anything and everything that comes to you is an important part of the Awakening Process. *Document everything!* This helps release energy and is helpful for you to look back and track your progress while also noticing your energetic patterns.

Other tools such as Tarot Cards and Oracle Cards can also assist with receiving Angelic Messages. When you are seeking Clarity, or you would like a Confirmation on something you are feeling, ask the Angels for 3 Confirmations. This is when you know it is the action/feeling that is in your best interest.

Here's an example:

If I feel into taking a certain action but am unsure, I ask my Angels for 3 Confirms. If I then see an *Angel Number* 3x, I accept that as Confirmation.

Angel Numbers are Synchronistic Numbers that hold meaning for us. The Angels use these as a way of communicating in the event we are unable to receive their guidance directly (due to stress, fear, spinning energy, or lack of feeling). The following are examples of Angel Numbers that appear as double, triple, our quadruple numbers:

Angel Number 111 is a direct message from your Angels to pay closer attention to your present self and your surroundings. *What do you see, and does it support you? Is it helping you or hurting you? What are your intentions?* Take full account of all you have, and change course, if required. It also serves as a re-hearter, so always pay close attention to your actions. Ask yourself, *are my actions and the intentions they come from heart-based?*

Angel Number 222 tells us to go within. It may be time to slow down, to surrender, to take each breath as it comes and go easy on yourself. Some inner work may be required, as dysfunction is the lower aspect to the energies of the Number 2. A strive for balance will help you better achieve success.

Angel Number 333 is a message from Mother God to loosen your grip on reality, to play and have more fun, to laugh and live life as a gift. So, bring more joy into your experience and express your inner voice. Some hands-on work is required to evolve into these higher energies. Get out of the house and get your creative skills to work … and don't forget to taste the rainbow while you're at it.

Angel Number 444 marks a cornerstone of your journey of evolutionary growth and awakening. Production is required to move forward from where you are, however, so let go of everything you think you know and allow the forces of nature to guide you.

Angel Number 555 suggests foundations are set for your future path. Be steady and conscious with every step you take, which will allow you to make better advancement towards the next step. Manifestations are coming your way, so be keen in your awareness as to what you are allowing into your reality, making sure your boundaries are firm and set. And don't forget to have fun doing whatever you engage in for yourself.

Angel Number 666 represents Unity. Love Connections are being granted, and you are strongly being urged to step into Unity/Oneness. Enable more Self-Love, connect with Source (Mom) and spread her grace into your community and families. Have compassion with yourself during this process and do not enable drama. Be firm in your values and your Service to Love.

Angel Number 777 is a definitive message that your Angels are listening to your prayers, and they are being fulfilled. 777 is considered to be a very lucky number, and casinos agree. But luck is simply not the case. In reality, the Universe is saying *"yes, this is yours"* and ushering you forward with passion, should you choose to act. Trust your intuition and continue listening to your guidance.

Angel Number 888 represents a completion of your karmic cycle, where two polar-opposite paths meet and intercept, to mirror each other for your self-transformation. Feel into this moment and breathe deeply into the experience, embracing whatever comes up. This is also a potent number that represents Manifestation and Abundance.

Angel Number 999 is a cosmic number indeed, and it says that, God heard you, she is opening her arms up to you. As the Universe, you are within. 999 represents a soul level-up of sorts, a peak in your evolution of consciousness. The 9 represents closure, soul completion, and a new phase beginning.

The Angel Messages are all suggesting your arrival to a new place on your Ascension Journey, so they offer you a good time to find and study all your notes, encouraging you to connect the dots and perhaps do even more research, if required.

Let Go and Move Forward with whatever information Source has gifted you through your Angels and Guides and put their information into action in your life. With perseverance and clear determination, your progress is imminent!

HOMEWORK

Sit down with a pen and paper and Connect with your Guides. You can use card decks or any other tool that assists you with getting their information. (That said, We DO NOT recommend tools such as pendulums, as they carry the lower vibration of manipulation.)

Ask the Angels anything you'd like! See what answer you get back. Feel their presence, ask them for a sign or message, and be observant of how they are communicating with you.

Notice any synchronistic numbers that are appearing for you. Reference our explanations, as well as many others, but only take what resonates with you.

Your Angels may also send your unique codes, such as, if you always see a certain number (like 625). This is how you know your Angels are directly sending YOU a message. *They enjoy codes!*

Feel into any question or something that you have been lacking clarity on, or anything you would like confirmation of. State it out loud to your Angels and ask them for 3 Confirmations. Then, notice what you are feeling into or are pinged on. Document your experiences and synchronicities over the next several days.

Angels also learn to communicate with you based on your unique way of receiving information. They may bring you a certain song (over and over again), a phrase or word found through articles or conversations, or they may bring you more playful messages like feathers or flowers! Learn what your favorite mode of communication is with your Angels.

COURSE 10: HEALING KARMIC DNA

As you begin to Dissolve Your EGO, Anchor In Your Higher Self, and Develop Your Intuition, your wounds will be coming up for Healing. This can feel painful, but it is a necessary part of the process. The Truth is that TRIGGERS ARE TREASURE.

When you are triggered, you Become Aware where you are still holding onto pain and suffering and EGO. Use your tools and techniques to Face These Wounds and Allow Them to Heal. As you Heal yourself, and your own wounding, you also begin Healing your Karmic DNA.

Scientists will often say that 90% of our DNA is "junk DNA". This is because the 90% is God Consciousness DNA, which cannot be understood by someone in the MIND, who is not at the level of Consciousness to comprehend it. The 10% of the DNA, which they can study, is the EGO-Programming. *Get it?* We can only comprehend things that are of the same Consciousness level.

The 10% of our DNA that is able to be studied and understood is our Karmic DNA. These are the survival mechanisms, the EGO-Programmings, and generational woundings that are passed from generation to generation. The Karmic DNA creates karmic loops, pain/illness/disease, and suffering.

This is why science claims that many diseases or dysfunctions are "genetic". There is no such thing as genetics, there is only frequency. When a being holds trauma, fear, pain and suffering, and it is untransformed, this will transfer to their baby upon its birth. Hence why many children end up suffering from the same "genetic" illnesses as their parents.

Once you begin Healing yourself, you assist in the Healing of everyone you are energetically connected to, including family, friends, partners, and children. The key to complete Healing of your Karmic DNA is to end the karmic loops. This means:

- -Taking accountability for YOUR dysfunction
- -Choosing to Evolve and Heal
- -Dissolving all blame, judgment, projection and externalization
- -Forgiving everyone and everything who has ever caused you pain or wounding
- -Accepting yourself and all experiences that you have chosen to have in this lifetime, and others
- -Leading by example

Once our Karmic DNA begins to Heal, it allows our God Consciousness DNA (the 90%) to activate.

HOMEWORK

Make a list of every moment in your life in which you felt hurt, wounded, or traumatized. It is not necessary to re-live the experience, just look at it from a place of Non-Attachment. Write down what you felt in the moment of that experience and write down how you feel about it now.

Next, also write down a list of any moment in your life when you hurt or wounded someone else, even if unintentionally. Write down how you felt about that experience then and how you feel about it now.

This may bring up a lot of stored guilt, anger, resentment, shame, judgment, or grief. Allow all of these emotions to come up. There is no reason to hold onto these emotions, as they are all just part of your Healing.

Now then, write a Forgiveness Ceremony for all of these events and people, including yourself, and burn it! Feel how freeing this is for you. (You may do this ceremony as many times as you need to, and keep in mind that, this process may come up many times.)

As you learn to Forgive all the people in your life, you also may be called to Draw Boundaries. Just because we Forgive and Unconditionally Love others does not mean that we allow their dysfunction to affect us. Use Discernment.

Remember that this is a process and does not happen overnight. TRUST THE PROCESS. When We Trust The Process, We Accept, Embrace And Allow All The Ebbs And Flows, Ups And Downs, And Lessons And Blessings.

We cannot control this process, nor can we rush it. You may often feel like you are going backwards, but you are not! Nothing is linear; everything moves in a spiral. When you feel you are hitting a wall, it's normally a test and a sign that you are actually leveling up! Once we reach a new level, we suddenly feel like we're struggling, but we are simply mastering that new level and that takes some practice!

Please refer to the Appendix with our sample **30 Day Self-Love Discipline Routine** that you may reference and utilize to integrate these disciplines into your daily life.

CONCLUSION

AS WE MOVE BEYOND TOGETHER …

We are so Grateful to all of you In The Heart who have read this book and are applying its Wisdoms. In many moments, from my personal experience, this Awakening Journey has been heartbreaking, infuriating, painful and excruciating. I have wanted to quit and throw in the towel thousands of times, yet my soul would not allow it. *Because within all the lows and chaos, there is profound beauty.*

My experience is unique because I had the honor and privilege of meeting Mother God in person, being trained by her, and witnessing the greatest example of Love I have ever known. The First Contact Ground Crew is my family, and we have found community around the globe with thousands of others who have chosen to stand up for Love, to embark on this wild journey, and to dedicate their lives to Serving Humanity and Anchoring In New Earth.

I will not tell you this journey is easy, because it isn't. *Once you Awaken, you can never go back to what you've known before. The old you, the old ways, and the old world will no longer resonate with you, and this can be scary and an extreme challenge for the human soul.*

I hope this book provides you the Strength, Support and Encouragement to keep going. No matter what, stay focused on the Truth that LOVE HAS WON, and Humanity is now returning to the

Light. Heaven on Earth is coming. It is here. Mom was our lighthouse, and she kept the light on at the end of the tunnel for us … we hope to do the same for all Humanity.

If you wish to connect with us further to learn, get guidance, collaborate, + connect, we have created numerous platforms and communities.

Our website **5Dfulldisclosure.org** is designed as a Light Center to provide you with everything you will need for this journey. We have a Library full of Beautiful Guides of Wisdom we have put together as well as videos that share our experience with these Tools, Techniques, and the Journey of Healing.

We have Sessions + Seminars available on our website to help provide Individual and Group Healing, Activations + Guidance for embodying your greatest and grandest version of yourself.

We also have a Podcast (that can be freely accessed) filled with amazing downloads and further insights into all the wisdom shared in this book.

We have built some Amazing Communities for those who are stepping into their Higher Self and want to help lead by example and Guide the Transition to New Earth. This includes our Telegram Channels + Our New Earth Transitionary Government.

Please check out our website and all that we have to offer, to You and to Humanity.

We Welcome ALL of You to Connect with Us. We are Always Here, In Service to Humanity and All of Creation.

With Love --- *Archeia Aurora*

APPENDIX

30 DAY SELF-LOVE DISCIPLINE PLAN

Day 1: Root Chakra Day

- Begin a garlic cleanse. 1 clove for 7 days. Chop garlic finely and let it air out for 15 mins, then take with food or by swallowing.
- Ground for 5 mins outside. Feet on the ground with deep breaths in through the nose and out through the mouth. If the temperature does not allow, use a grounding mat inside.
- Write down 10 things you are grateful for

Day 2: Sacral Chakra Day

- Choose 1 creative outlet for the day (i.e., painting, drawing, dancing, cooking, etc.)
- Move your body for 45 mins (walking, running, yoga, dancing, etc.)
- Journal 10 mins about how you are feeling and what is coming up for you

Day 3 Solar Plexus Day

- Choose 20 Divine Traits and practice Mirror Affirmations beginning with *I AM*
- Practice blessing your food and water using the prayer: *"Thank you, Mother Earth, for this food, thank you to the animals, farmers and preparers of this food. I ask for this food to be transformed into the highest organic ingredients of Love, light and rainbow energy"*
- Drink 8-10 glasses of blessed water

Day 4 Heart Chakra Day

- Write down all the things you are still holding onto – hurt, regrets, guilt, shame, resentments, grief, etc. Write these all down on a piece of paper and then write out a letter of forgiveness for all the experiences, for yourself and all others involved. Burn this in a ceremony with the intent to clear this heavy energy.
- Spend 30 minutes on Self-Care – a shower or bath meditation, drinking tea, lighting a candle, reading a book, etc. Whatever brings you joy and comfort.
- Practice Breathwork. 2-3 minutes of breathing in deeply through the nose with Love, letting it fill your body, then breathing out through the mouth, releasing all density.

Day 5 Throat Chakra Day

- Play music and sing out loud to your favorite songs

- Write a ceremony of all your dreams and manifestations for New Earth. Read it out loud and burn it.
- Make your favorite tea (can include turmeric, coconut oil, or cinnamon, for added clearing)

Day 6 Third Eye Chakra Day

- Write an EGO Death Ceremony. Write down all the programming you know that you have and/or are still struggling to dissolve. Burn this in a ceremony with the intent to dissolve these programmings.
- 10-15 of Meditation. This can be guided meditation or using music, if preferred. Focus on filling your body with rainbow light and activating all dormant parts of your DNA.
- Practice Praying with Intent before going to sleep and asking your Angels to help you sleep consciously and process energy through your rest. Ask your Angels to wake you up when it is highest for you to get up and see what happens!

Day 7 Crown Chakra Day

- Sit down for 10 minutes and practice Automatic Writing with your Angels & Higher Self. Ask for all information or guidance to come through and write down whatever comes to you.
- Practice the mantra *"I cut cords with everyone and everything and all events. I re-attach all my energetic cords with everything whole, pure, true and in resonance with Love."* Then use the mantra *"I return all energy that is not mine or in my Highest Good to the Sender."*
- Finish your 7-day garlic cleanse

- Journal for 10-15 mins about any synchronistic events or happenings from your week. Write down anything you feel is important for you to look back on.

Day 8 Root Chakra Day

- Cleanse your space. Choose one room of the house, or your entire house, and cleanse all spaces (especially bedrooms). Finish by saging the space or using incense/candles/wax melts to assist in setting new energies.
- Cook a meal using red meat. Bless the meat and all ingredients as you cook. Ask the Angels to ping you on what ingredients to use and how much. Enjoy your grounding meal.
- Stretch your body for 10-15 minutes

Day 9 Sacral Chakra Day

- Write down your earliest memory of experiencing trauma or an event that you always remember that created fear, hurt, or pain for you. Then write down how these experiences still affect you to this day. Burn this piece of paper and ask it all to be released.
- Write a letter to your inner child, giving them encouragement, Love, and guidance, speaking as your future self.
- Use the mantra, *"I'm sorry, please forgive me, thank you, I Love you."*

Day 10 Solar Plexus Day

- Sun Gaze for 5 minutes or as long as you are able to.
- Fast for at least 10 hours of the day. Drink only – water, tea, juice, etc. Fasting will assist the body in resetting and clearing the greatest amount of density.
- *I AM* Affirmations in the mirror

Day 11 Heart Chakra Day

- Write a Love Letter to yourself and keep it with you to reference back to
- Do a shower or bath meditation. Bless the water and ask for all density to be released and cleansed from your vessel
- Do a Heart Chakra meditation. Envision your heart being filled with golden rainbow light, expanding more and more until you feel you have reached your current capacity. Allow yourself to release through crying, if you need to.

Day 12 Throat Chakra Day

- Write down your reflections from the last week and what you are feeling
- Eat blue/purple foods such as berries or potatoes
- Choose someone in your life you feel you need to express something to. This could be a Truth, how you really feel, or something you feel needs to be expressed. You can do this verbally or written.

Day 13 Third Eye Chakra Day

- Ask your Angels for guidance or information on anything you are looking for clarity on. Ask them for 3 Confirmations and then write down any syncs or confirms that you receive. Allow the answers to come organically.
- Write down all of the things you imagine New Earth to be like, everything you dream of.
- Write another EGO Death Ceremony using the same programmings (or additional ones) you feel coming up. Burn it with the intent of releasing a deeper layer.

Day 14 Crown Chakra Day

- Rest today
- Use this day as a day of staying calm, keeping activity to a minimum and relaxing. The art of "just being" may raise uncomfortable feelings of "needing to do something". If this occurs, breathe through the uncomfortableness by allowing yourself to enjoy this rest.
- Watch your favorite show or movie

Day 15 Root Chakra Day

- Ground outside with your bare feet on the ground for at least 10 minutes. If the temperature does not allow for this, utilize a mat indoors and envision yourself grounding into the Earth.
- Write down a goal list of anything you wish to accomplish in the next 15 days. Put it where you can see it each day.

- Utilize the red flame for 10-15 minutes and envision it purifying your Root Chakra of all fear, lack, or instability. Allow any feelings to come to the surface and then release them.

Day 16 Sacral Chakra Day

- Write down a list of everything that brings you joy. Feel into each item on your list and whether it is a want, need or desire, and document if whatever it is truly fulfills your soul. Commit to doing something each day that brings you joy.
- Do one creative practice today (painting, dancing, cooking, drawing, designing, etc.)
- Watch a comedy show or movie that will make you laugh.

Day 17 Solar Plexus Day

- Drink a glass of lemon water in the morning (with apple cider vinegar) to help cleanse your stomach from toxins
- Write down your greatest passions or what inspires you. Ask your Angels how you can take daily steps towards living your passions & inspirations.
- *I AM* Affirmations

Day 18 Heart Chakra Day

- Write down all the ways in which you have Served Love the past two weeks. Compare this list to your passions, inspirations, dreams and to-do list. *How do these align or not align?* Service to Love is also Self-Love.

- Make a Heart Chakra smoothie or yogurt bowl filled with berries, greens, and coconut oil.
- 30 minutes of Self-Care (anything your body and soul is asking for to bring comfort and nurturing to your body and soul).

Day 19 Throat Chakra Day

- Speak your Truth to at least one person today. This means that you do not hold back, stuff anything down, or censor yourself, but rather, you allow yourself to speak your Truth, no matter how uncomfortable the situation makes you. Ask your Angels to bring you the opportunity to do so.
- Say out loud 3x, *"Bring it on, Angels!"*
- Record a message to yourself documenting your experiences and keep it on your phone to refer back to. Speaking out loud and listening back to your voice can help you see what frequencies are coming through your voice.

Day 20 Third Eye Chakra Day

- 10-15 minutes of Meditation, visualizing your body being filled with light, and the entire planet being filled with light and healing. Send Love to all of Humanity.
- Turmeric tea and coconut oil.
- Do an EGO Death Ceremony for all remaining EGO-Programmings affecting you and ask for all spiritual and superego aspects to be cleared from your vessel.

Day 21 Crown Chakra Day

- Journal 10-15 minutes about your reflections of the week and how you have been feeling, noting all that has come up for you. Then, refer back to all your reflections of the past 3 weeks.
- Play your favorite music and ask the Angels to bring you codes or downloads through the music.
- Take a shower meditation or bath meditation and cleanse all energies coming up for you.

Day 22 Root Chakra Day

- Cleanse your space again and utilize sage, incense or candles to help set a higher vibration for your space. Get rid of all your clutter! Donate what you don't need to allow space for new things to come into manifestation.
- Write down what you wish to manifest into your life and burn the list.
- Make a meal with red meat, blessing each ingredient and asking for Angel guidance on what to create and what ingredients to use.

Day 23 Sacral Chakra Day

- Write down and reflect on all relationship dysfunction you have had in your life. Read the control dramas from the *Ascension Guide* and feel into how these control dramas have played a role in your relationships and life.

- Write a Forgiveness Ceremony for all relationship wounding to be released. Write letters of forgiveness to yourself and past partners. This allows all things you wish you would have said to be put down on paper and then dissolved and healed.
- Choose your favorite food and create a delicious meal for yourself (and family, if applicable). Set the table as if you are having a celebration.

Day 24 Solar Plexus Day

- Drink 8-10 glasses of blessed water.
- Sun Gaze for 10 minutes.
- Choose 20 new Divine Traits & do your *I AM* Mirror Affirmations

Day 25 Heart Chakra Day

- Write down 10 things you are grateful for
- Read the Love letter you wrote to yourself earlier in the month. Write a second Love Letter to yourself to reference next month.
- Give someone you Love a gift! This can be an act of service, a physical gift from your heart, a Love Letter, some kind words, or a hug.

Day 26 Throat Chakra Day

- Write a ceremony asking for all blocks to Divine Listening to be removed. Focus on truly listening as others speak to you and begin to feel the frequencies of their words, rather than the words themselves. Write down your observations of the frequencies you observe in others' speech and reflect on your own.
- Smile at every person you see today, or call someone you haven't spoken to for a while and ask them how they are doing.
- Listen to the recording you made last week of your experiences. Reflect on how you feel and what you observe from the recording today. Record a second one of your current experiences to reference next time.

Day 27 Third Eye Day

- Do a right brain activation meditation by focusing on rainbow light entering your right brain and fully activating all neurons. Then, see it connecting the right and left brain together. Feel into the sensations that arise.
- Write down all Divine Traits, beginning with the *I AM*s, using the opposite hand that you normally would. This helps activate the right side of the brain.
- Watch a show or movie that inspires you.

Day 28 Crown Chakra Day

- Do Automatic Writing with your Higher Self and Angels for 10-15 minutes.
- Write down your reflections of the past month and refer back to what you have been experiencing the last few weeks.

- Review your To-Do List and see what you were able to accomplish, as well as look at how your dreams, passions and inspirations may have shifted and changed.
- Create a 30-day plan for yourself for the next month using your favorite disciplines and tools that resonate with you. Feel free to switch these up as you feel guided!

ABOUT THE AUTHOR

A. Aurora was born and raised in South Florida and spent the majority of her life in academia. She has been studying Astrology, Energy, Metaphysics, and Spirituality for the past 14 years. Through leaps of faith and synchronistic events, her heart led her onto a path of awakening that ultimately guided her to finding her greatest Teacher, Mother of All Creation. She studied and was trained by Mother for over 3 years and her journey has now led her to dedicating her life in service to Humanity, to help them awaken, heal, and remember who they truly are – God with God.

BOOKS BY THE AUTHOR

5D Full Disclosure: Whole Truth Heals

Children's Books:

The Tree of Life: A Creation Story

MORE COMING SOON!

Made in United States
North Haven, CT
24 July 2025